PARIS MODERN: THE SWEDISH BALLET 1920–1925

BALLETS SUÉDOIS

M Vassilieff

JEAN BORLIN

PARIS MODERN

THE SWEDISH BALLET 1920–1925

Nancy Van Norman Baer

with contributions by
Jan Torsten Ahlstrand
William Camfield
Judi Freeman
Lynn Garafola
Gail Levin
Robert M. Murdock
Erik Näslund
Anna Greta Ståhle

FINE ARTS MUSEUMS OF SAN FRANCISCO
Distributed by the University of Washington Press

This book has been published in conjunction with the exhibition *Paris Modern: The Swedish Ballet 1920-1925*.

The Museum at the Fashion Institute of Technology
New York, New York
9 October 1995–15 January 1996

The McNay Art Museum
San Antonio, Texas
12 February–12 May 1996

Fine Arts Museums of San Francisco
15 June–September 8 1996

The exhibition and catalogue are made possible by support from the National Endowment for the Arts, a Federal agency; the Bernard Osher Foundation; the Rolf de Maré Foundation; Franklin/Templeton Funds; and the American-Scandinavian Foundation. SAS Airline provided transportation for the exhibition.

First published in 1995 by the Fine Arts Museums of San Francisco.
Distributed by the University of Washington Press, Seattle.

Library of Congress No. 95-61830
ISBN 0-88401-081-3

COVER:
Fernand Léger, set design with three godlike figures for *La Creation du monde* (detail), 1923, cat. no. 79.

PAGE 1:
Audrey Parr, costume design for the Cymbals in *L'Homme et son désir*, 1921, cat. no. 110.

PAGE 2:
Marie Vasilieff, program cover design for Ballets Suédois, ca. 1924, cat. no. 138.

PAGE 168:
Eldsten, design for poster, Ballets Suédois, ca. 1921, cat. no. 27.

All illustrations, unless noted otherwise, are in the collection of the Dansmuseet, Stockholm.

Exceptions are on pages 115, figure 6; 116, figure 8; and 133, figure 3. The locations of these images are unknown.

Printed and bound in Hong Kong

Contents

Preface

The Swedish Ballet, headquartered in Paris as the Ballets Suédois from 1920 to 1925, boldly challenged conventional conceptions of dance with its innovative, multidisciplinary approach. The company's collaborators represented every significant artistic tendency of the early twentieth century, including postimpressionism, symbolism, expressionism, cubism, and dada. *Paris Modern: The Swedish Ballet 1920-1925* enables us to recapture the excitement of the company's trendsetting performances.

Although the Ballets Suédois survived for a mere five years, its revolutionary productions altered the course of dance history. Aware of the significance of its innovations, Rolf de Maré, founder and director of the company, established Les Archives Internationales de la Danse (AID) to preserve the legacy of its historic but ephemeral creations. Unfortunately the AID, one of the world's first dance museums, did not survive the Second World War. The AID collection was ultimately broken up and dispersed between the Dansmuseet in Stockholm and the Bibliothèque de l'Opéra de Paris.

Alma de Bretteville Spreckels, founder of the California Palace of the Legion of Honor, retained a vivid memory of her enchanting afternoon at the AID in Paris in 1937. According to an interview published in the *San Francisco Examiner*, that fortuitous visit inspired Mrs. Spreckels to establish a museum of theater and dance in San Francisco. The lower floor of her Washington Street mansion served as the site for this museum until the collection outgrew those quarters. The costume and set designs, sculpture, and drawings from Alma Spreckels's fledgling dance museum now form the nucleus of the Fine Arts Museums of San Francisco's Theater and Dance Collection.

Alma Spreckels would be doubly pleased if she were alive today. Not only has a recently completed seismic upgrading and renovation program given the California Palace of the Legion of Honor a new lease on life, but the Legion is celebrating its reopening by including a major dance-related exhibit in its first exhibition season. We are delighted to share this project with two participating cultural institutions. Thanks to the cooperation of our colleagues Dorothy Twining Globus at The Museum at the Fashion Institute of Technology in New York City, and William J. Chiego at The McNay Art Museum in San Antonio, wide-ranging American audiences will be able to appreciate the innovations of the Ballets Suédois for the first time since that company toured the United States in 1923-24.

We are most grateful to the Dansmuseet in Stockholm and to its director Erik Näslund for their generosity and collaboration. This exhibition features some two-

Fig. 1
PIERRE BONNARD
(Fontenay-aux-Roses, France 1867–1947 Cannet, France)
Set design for *Jeux*, 1920
Pastel on paper, 51 x 65 cm

Fernand Léger, Joan Miró, and Pablo Picasso, as well as an El Greco masterpiece. De Maré's passion for art grew naturally out of his family background: As a young boy he had been allowed to help choose paintings for the collection assembled by his grandmother, the Countess Wilhelmina von Hallwyl. De Maré's love for modern art arose later from his close friendship with the Swedish painter Nils Dardel, who had been a student of Henri Matisse in Paris.

Given de Maré's strong interest in painting, the intentional pictorial emphasis of Ballets Suédois productions is hardly surprising. In a metaphorical sense the underwriting of new ballets allowed de Maré to collect the modern art movement itself in addition to individual works of art. With the Ballets Suédois he created an artistic refuge for himself and others, one that because of his family's wealth was not dependent on box-office receipts or the whims of patrons. In 1924 the painter Francis Picabia described the impresario's enthusiasm for dance and his unique contribution:

[De Maré] loves the ballets, his ballets: he says so; he proves it. He wants to infuse them with more life, novelty, and strength; and his work has a much greater importance than even he himself thinks. It permits an entire cosmopolitan generation in Paris to work with a purpose, with the possibility of expressing itself freely, without the paralyzing worry of what should or should not please.[2]

Because movement was often subordinated to stage design, one might argue that the Ballets Suédois was not really a dance company in any traditional sense but rather a group dedicated to performance and installation art. When the company toured the United States in 1923 newspapers sent a variety of critics—drama, music, painting, and otherwise (there were virtually no American dance critics per se at the time)—to cover the performances. In Syracuse, New York, the task fell to the sports editor, who described the production of the folklore ballet *Nuit de Saint Jean* (Saint John's Night, or Midsummer Night's Revel) as an "amateur athletic entertainment" featuring a "free-for-all wrestling match" with "strangle holds and bar-Nelsons in evidence"![3]

In formulating his plans for a company de Maré realized that the presentation of new dance ideas in Sweden would be obstructed by the inert tradition and conven-

Fig. 2
Jeux, Paris, 1920, cat. no. 183.

tional prejudice that then prevailed. He therefore chose Paris—the capital of the avant-garde art world—as the headquarters for his enterprise.[4] Paris amply met de Maré's needs for creative collaborators, a supportive artistic atmosphere, and an appropriate performance space, the Théâtre des Champs-Elysées. But there may have been another reason for de Maré's decision to headquarter his company in the French capital. Its permissive society allowed him to express his homoerotic preference. In Sweden such behavior would have embarrassed some of his friends and relatives. Events proved him right; in spite of the fact that he went abroad, de Maré's enterprise was criticized in Sweden because the Ballets Suédois had been founded in protest against the old-fashioned regime and bureaucratic principles of the Royal Opera in Stockholm.

In early 1918 de Maré was introduced to one of Sweden's most gifted young dancers, Jean Börlin (1893–1930), with whom he soon became sexually involved. Börlin had received his early training at the ballet school of Stockholm's Royal Opera. It was there that he was singled out by the Russian choreographer Michel Fokine who, after resigning from Diaghilev's Ballets Russes in 1913, had been invited to Sweden to assume the role of guest choreographer at the Royal Opera. Fokine introduced the Diaghilev repertory to Sweden and taught Börlin both at the Opera and in a private studio in Copenhagen. Many years later Fokine recalled his first impression of the dancer:

He crossed the stage with great bounds, landed with all his weight and glided over the boards among the group of bacchantes. What character! What ecstasy! The fanatical sacrifice of a bruised body in order to produce the maximum of choreographic effect.[5]

Following Börlin's early death in 1930 Fokine wrote:

Börlin was the one who resembled me most and who corresponded to the ideal I had of a dancer.[6]

It was the young dancer's exceptional talent as well as his sexual relationship with de Maré that led to Börlin's appointment as choreographer, ballet master, and principal dancer for the Ballets Suédois. The choice was fortunate. Börlin brought not only talent and dance technique to the enterprise but a profound sympathy with the visual arts. In an interview Börlin stated:

Fig. 3
THÉOPHILE ALEXANDRE STEINLEN
Costume design for a Spanish Dancer in *Iberia*, 1920, cat. no. 133.

Fig. 4
THÉOPHILE ALEXANDRE STEINLEN
Costume design for a Sailor in *Iberia*, 1920, cat. no. 131.

Each painting that moves me is transformed in me into dance. . . . [Although] rhythm will always remain the principal and most mysterious element of choreographic creation, painting can be the point of departure [for] the first inspiration.[7]

Börlin's dominant role within the company allowed him to enforce stylistic consistency. Reviewers commented on the static, pantomimic quality of movement and friezelike compositions that characterized many of the Ballets Suédois productions. In discussing the refinement and taste of Börlin's vision one historian observed:

The Swedish Ballet departs entirely from the Asiatic, gorgeous, half-barbaric and decidedly erotic style [of the Russian Ballet] as much as it does from conventional platitude. . . . It desires something more than merely dancing, technical capacity and masterly execution; it desires to give expression to a thought, an idea. It also desires to interpret the inner life—the emotion of the human soul.[8]

In contrast to Börlin's single choreographic voice, thirty-two painters representing eleven nationalities designed and executed the costumes and backdrops for the twenty-three ballets produced during the company's existence. Their works represented, in varying degree, virtually every artistic style of the period.

The visual artists commissioned by de Maré tended to treat the stage as if it were a canvas, with the proscenium arch serving as a frame. Their painted backdrops were animated by Börlin's frontal choreography. Archival photographs suggest that the two-dimensional quality was reinforced by the confinement of much of the danced movement to the front of the stage. The visual effect was that of a painting with moving elements. This pictorial quality caused one historian to remark:

In the Ballets Suédois, painting became invasive. Some ballets were true plastic exhibitions, with the entire stage monopolized by the painter; the dancer became almost [superfluous]. A new formula of spectacle was born.[9]

De Maré played fairly safe in programming his company's Paris debut. The first Ballets Suédois performance consisted of four works that the impresario himself described as "ballets sages"—prudent ballets:[10]

Taking thoroughly into account my little experience, [and] in spite of my desire for innovation, I called upon musicians and painters [who were] called "advanced" but [who had already been] recognized.[11]

Among these relatively traditional pieces was Börlin's new version of *Jeux* (Games), with music by Claude

Debussy, presented in front of an impressionist backdrop created by the well-known painter Pierre Bonnard (Figs. 1–2). The couturiere Jeanne Lanvin designed the costumes for the ballet, which was originally choreographed in 1913 by Vaslav Nijinsky for Diaghilev's Ballets Russes. A pleasant and harmonious production, it was said to lack the seduction and mysterious poetry of Nijinsky's version, even though it created a "shimmering impression."[12]

A much-loved painter, Théophile Alexandre Steinlen, designed *Iberia*, which appeared on the same program. Performed to the music of Isaac Albéniz, it was described by a reviewer as a "mélange of voluptuous dances" evoking "the activity of a Spanish port, the fever of a gypsy quarter, and the voluptuous pleasure of religious Seville." Critics remarked that Börlin's choreography was more modern than traditional, and they credited the corps de ballet for dancing "with ardor and passion without being frenetic."[13]

Steinlen's backdrops and costumes were executed from loosely rendered designs that suggest a stylized reality (Figs. 3–4). The backdrop for act 1 depicts a Spanish port with boats and riggings rendered in an exaggerated scale, while the dark entrance to a cave, the focal point in the backdrop for act 2, captures the furtive nature of gypsy life (Figs. 5–6). The latter design is especially interesting for dance historians because it includes the representation of a low platform table on which a woman in Spanish costume dances. In 1928 this image would be realized three-dimensionally in Bronislava Nijinska's production of *Bolero*, created for the Ida Rubinstein Ballet (Figs. 7–8).[14]

The company's inaugural program continued with *Nuit de Saint Jean*, designed by Dardel with music by the Swedish composer Hugo Alfvén. Inspired by Swedish folklore and created by a team of Swedish collaborators, this lighthearted ballet included dances performed around a maypole. The primary colors and flattened perspective of Dardel's backdrop also reflected folk-art influences.

Audiences responded with enthusiasm to *Nuit de Saint Jean* because of its relative accessibility and its assertion of the company's national identity. A charming ballet, it was performed "in an amiable burlesque style" and featured "rouged faces, gauche and rude gestures, and the uninhibited fun of a peasant celebration."[15] The dance sequences were derived entirely from the steps and movement style of Swedish folk dance, which had been translated by Börlin into an abstract folk choreography. One critic summed it up as "a perfect evocation of the Northern 'primitive.'"[16]

Fig. 5
THÉOPHILE ALEXANDRE STEINLEN
Set design for Act 1 of *Iberia:* The Port, 1920, cat. no. 128.

Fig. 6
THÉOPHILE ALEXANDRE STEINLEN
Set design for Act 2 of *Iberia:* Albaicin, 1920, cat. no. 129.

Fig. 7
ALEXANDRE BENOIS
Set design for *Bolero*, 1928
Pencil and watercolor on paper, 26.6 x 35.5 cm
Collection Nina Youshkevitch, New York

Fig. 8
Bolero, Paris, 1928
Nijinska Archives, Pacific Palisades, California

The company's high spirits were reflected during a performance that took place one month after the ballet's premiere. The dancers and Börlin himself were startled to see an unknown man appear with them onstage. Wearing a green overcoat and high-crowned hat, he sat down at the table where the peasants were pretending to eat and drink. As one critic reported,

the dancers had not reached the end of their surprise. The huge goblets of wood, usually empty, were this night full of good wine, and the "property cakes" had been replaced by a large and appetizing pastry. The dancers ate and drank, to the immense stupefaction of M. de Maré, who, standing in the wings, did not know what to make of it.

At the moment when the peasants begin a mad dance about a May-pole, the man in the green coat joined hands with the others and entered fully into their gaiety. The ballet ended tempestuously—and then, to the amazement of all, it was recognized that the man in the green coat was no other than the painter Steinlen, who had chosen this way of making his debut as a dancer.[17]

The final work to be presented on the first program was *Derviches* (Dervishes), with music by Alexander Glazunov and a decor by the Paris Opéra's head scene painter, Georges Mouveau, in the style of an Indian miniature.[18] This danced interlude was performed in traditional costume and accurately reproduced the movement of whirling dervishes. *Derviches* met with mixed response. Some critics praised its "sumptuous simplicity," describing the piece as "a corner of hot India with golden dervishes that turn and turn," while others saw it as being merely an exercise in rotation.[19]

While there was nothing revolutionary about the

Swedish Ballet's premiere program, it did establish the company as a legitimate artistic enterprise and announced an intention to present works of contemporary painters and musicians within a choreographed spectacle. It was the second and third programs of the first Paris season that signaled the company's willingness to venture outside the bounds of traditional ballet by offering two innovative works, *Maison de fous* (Madhouse) and *El Greco*.

Like *Nuit de Saint Jean*, *Maison de fous* was created by an entirely Swedish team of collaborators, which included the young composer Viking Dahl, a student of Maurice Ravel's in Paris; the future Nobel laureate Pär Lagerkvist, who wrote the libretto; Dardel, who designed the costumes and sets; and Börlin.

In devising his choreography for *Maison de fous*, Börlin asked members of the company to improvise movements appropriate to the characters they portrayed. He then selected and stylized their gestures to make an effective dance composition. Dardel's backdrop, depicting an anguished man of monstrous appearance with upraised arms and hands, was described as being "not a decor, but an hallucination" (Fig. 9).[20] In front of this image of torment the dancers, representing lunatics in an asylum, expressed grotesquely exaggerated emotions—aggression, confusion, obsession, hysteria, and despair (Fig. 10).

Much of the audience was not ready for this range of emotion on the ballet stage, and critics termed the production "lamentable" and "macabre."[21] Nevertheless, *Maison de fous* represented an important step in the evolution of modern ballet. Dance was no longer limited to the expression of romantic longings or exotic beauty; it was also capable of expressing the horrific aspects of contemporary society.

Another unusual work, based on the paintings of the Spanish mannerist El Greco, further inflamed the scandal created by *Maison de fous*. Like the earlier ballet this work conveyed a sense of anguish softened by a Mediterranean spirituality. The backdrop, created by Georges Mouveau, synthesized the line and color of El Greco's most famous works (Fig. 11).

El Greco featured Börlin in a series of mimed scenes in which he wore only a loincloth. His contorted gestures and expressions of suffering conveyed the spirit of El Greco's paintings, while his static poses and brilliantly positioned torso and legs displayed the choreographer's own extraordinary sense of line (Fig. 12). More than one critic commented on the subtle harmony and profound beauty of the ballet, and Börlin was praised for his ability to "interpret [El Greco's paintings] without betraying them."[22]

In the first three weeks of the company's existence the Ballets Suédois presented eight new ballets and one pas de deux, each in a different style. In addition to the works mentioned above there was *Le Tombeau de Couperin* (The Tomb of Couperin), a suite of dances based on eighteenth-century court forms that included "a languorous forlane, a tender and mischievious minuet, and an impertinent, robust rigaudon."[23] Maurice Ravel wrote the music for *Tombeau* in memory of the composer François Couperin (1668–1733). The ballet was performed in front of a painted French garden setting designed by Pierre Laprade.

The first-season repertory also included *Pas de deux*, set to music by Frédéric Chopin, and *Les Vierges folles* (The Foolish Virgins), a second ballet inspired by Swedish folk legend. As with *Nuit de Saint Jean* and *Maison de fous* this production was created by a group of Swedish collaborators, including the composer Kurt Atterburg and the painter Einar Nerman. Based on a biblical parable, *Les Vierges folles* was said to have the delicacy, charm, and color of an illuminated manuscript, and critics were delighted by its romantic portrayal of Nordic tradition.[24]

In programming these first performances de Maré and Börlin were sensitive to their audience, defying convention in one ballet while offering reassurance in another. Provocative works such as *Maison de fous* and *El Greco* were balanced by the Swedish folklore pieces, in which a childlike sense of innocence was preserved. In theatricalizing Swedish rural life and culture, ballets like *Nuit de Saint Jean* and *Les Vierges folles* provided a respite from modern life by evoking an idealized, harmonious past. The company's repertory allowed audiences to glimpse other exotic and distant cultures such as those of India, Spain, and Africa, albeit safely packaged to confirm preconceptions about foreigners.

During the 1921 season four new productions were added to the repertory, two relatively unchallenging works and two ballets that proclaimed de Maré's decision to "accept the risks of a more perilous exploration."[25] In clear oppostion to the *ballets sages*, these two vanguard works—*L'Homme et son désir* (Man and His Desire) and *Les Mariés de la Tour Eiffel* (The Newlyweds on the Eiffel Tower)—confirmed the company's intention to create theatrical spectacles in which all aspects of a production, including the choreography, were subordinated to the mise en scène.

The first example of this completely pictorial emphasis can be found in *L'Homme et son désir*, a collaboration between the French poet and playwright Paul Claudel,

Fig. 9
Nils Dardel
Backdrop design for *Maison de fous*, 1920, cat. no. 23.

Fig. 10
Maison de fous, Paris, 1920, cat. no. 190.

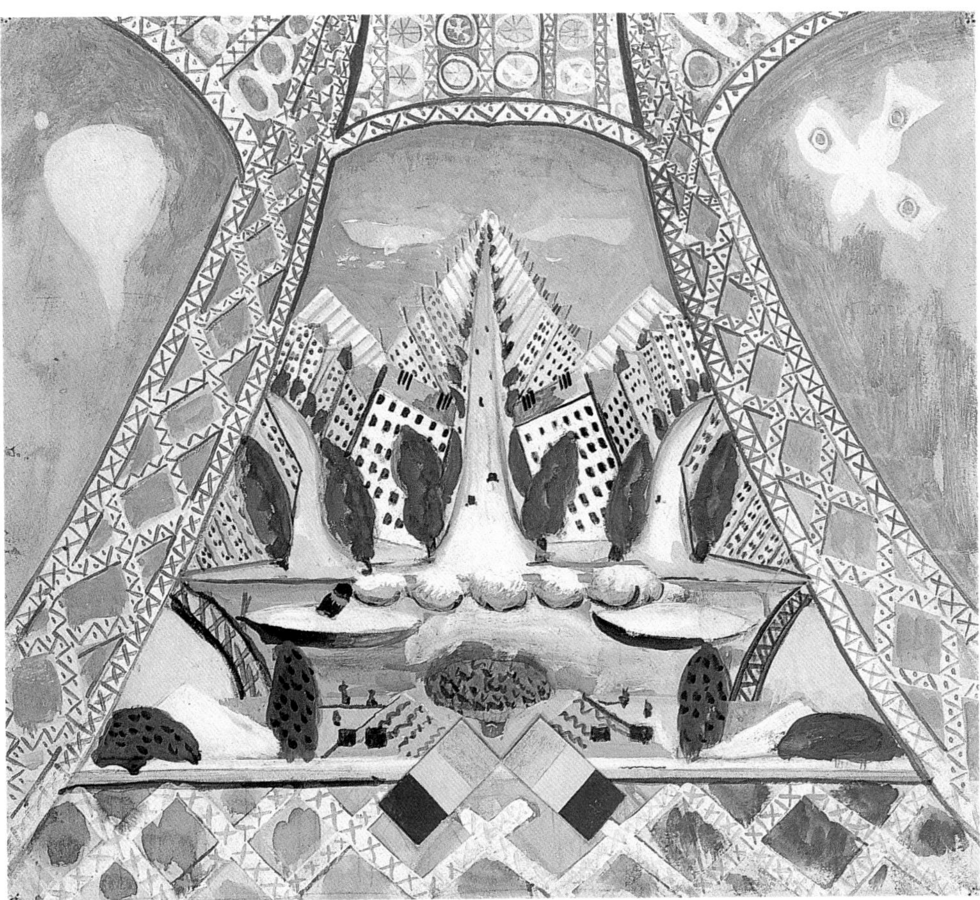

Fig. 18
IRÈNE LAGUT
Set design for *Les Mariés de la Tour Eiffel*, 1921, cat. no. 54.

Les Mariés de la Tour Eiffel allowed Cocteau to introduce spoken text, delivered through giant horns by hidden vocalists, to the ballet stage—an idea rejected by Diaghilev in 1917 for his production of *Parade* (Fig. 17). It also confirmed the company's pursuit of contemporary expression through its borrowings from popular culture. *Les Mariés de la Tour Eiffel* was not a ballet in any conventional sense, but a mixture of acrobatics, cabaret, circus, comedy, dance, drama, magic, music-hall, and pantomime.

The Eiffel Tower and the phonograph were not the only symbols of modern technology in the production; the camera also played a major part. This mechanical apparatus, which is supposed to capture an image of reality, in this instance supplied its own subject (through the various characters who emerged from its lens) and then literally captured it (the characters disappear back into the camera as the photograph is made).

Lagut's decor created a view from the Eiffel Tower that was described by an American reviewer as looking as if "a mad cubist was having a nightmare," with the various elements "all jazzed up and twisting about and running into one another" (Fig. 18).[32] It was also an American critic that referred to the group of musicians mentioned above, who composed the ballet's modern music and were known as Les Six, as the "sicks" (Fig. 19).[33]

The costume constructions and oversized masks worn by the dancers helped create the absurd and illogical world of *Les Mariés de la Tour Eiffel* (Figs. 20–21). Hugo and his fiancée, Valentine Gross, used wire frames and padding to create the exaggerated features and theatrical personalities of various characters, ranging from an ostrich to a hunchbacked photographer. Because the encumbered dancers were limited in movement and could barely hear the spoken dialogue or music, their gestures had to be precisely specified and timed. Their relatively static performance was animated by the few characters whose costumes did allow them to dance freely, such as the Bathing Girl and the Radio Telegrams, whose pointe work and ensemble groupings discreetly parodied the classical ballet.

Cocteau praised de Maré and Börlin for their understanding of his intentions and their daring in creating a new genre of theater that reflected the modern spirit.

Fig. 19
The group of musicians known as *Les Six:* (left to right) Germaine Tailleferre, Francis Poulenc, Arthur Honegger, Darius Milhaud, Louis Durey, Georges Auric, Paris, 1921, cat. no. 208.

As he explained, this new form of moving spectacle "will render the greatest service to France. . . . [It] will correct its slowness in shedding routine habits. . . and will show us, astonishing to ourselves, in a mirror as pure as the ice of the North."[34] Cocteau described the drama enacted in *Les Mariés de la Tour Eiffel* as being both ridiculous and truthful. As he explained:

Instead of seeking to refrain from the ridicule of life, instead of toning it down or [re]arranging it. . . I emphasize and seek to [portray] what is truer than the truth.[35]

The single new creation of 1922 was *Skating Rink*, with eye-catching cubist designs by the most eminent painter to be associated with the Ballets Suédois, Fernand Léger. This production, based on a poem by Ricciotto Canudo and with music by Honegger, embodied many of the principles advocated by Léger in his article "The Spectacle: Light, Color, Moving Image, Object-Spectacle." Among these were speed and brevity, in keeping with Léger's theory that "a spectacle must be fast-moving for the sake of its unity. It cannot go on for more that fifteen or twenty minutes."[36]

Skating Rink introduced an urban as well as modern theme to ballet, presenting a cross-section of human life, including workers and fashionable types, engaged in a popular pastime. The circular arena stood for the panorama of life, which was in itself the material of art. "On the asphalt of the skating rink turns the circle of the damned, compelled, by the roller skates, to a uniform movement. . . ," wrote the critic André Levinson.[37]

Léger's drop curtain provided a pictorial equivalent for the complex patterns of motion created by the dancers onstage. Overlapping geometric shapes and figurative elements were forced together in a barely differentiated unity. The backdrop, slightly curved to embrace the dancers and suggest the perimeter of the rink, was horizontally composed and divided into two distinct zones: the upper, a frieze of interlocking, flat, multicolored forms and the lower, a spatially neutral background for the mobile dancers (Fig. 22). Léger's design resulted in the first completely abstract ballet decor to be realized, and followed earlier experiments in abstract theater design by George Appia, Edward Gordon Craig, Kazimir Malevich, Giacomo Balla, and Fortunato Depero.

The costumes for *Skating Rink* applied the geometry of the decor to the figures of the dancers, creating a kaleidoscopic sequence of images that changed accord-

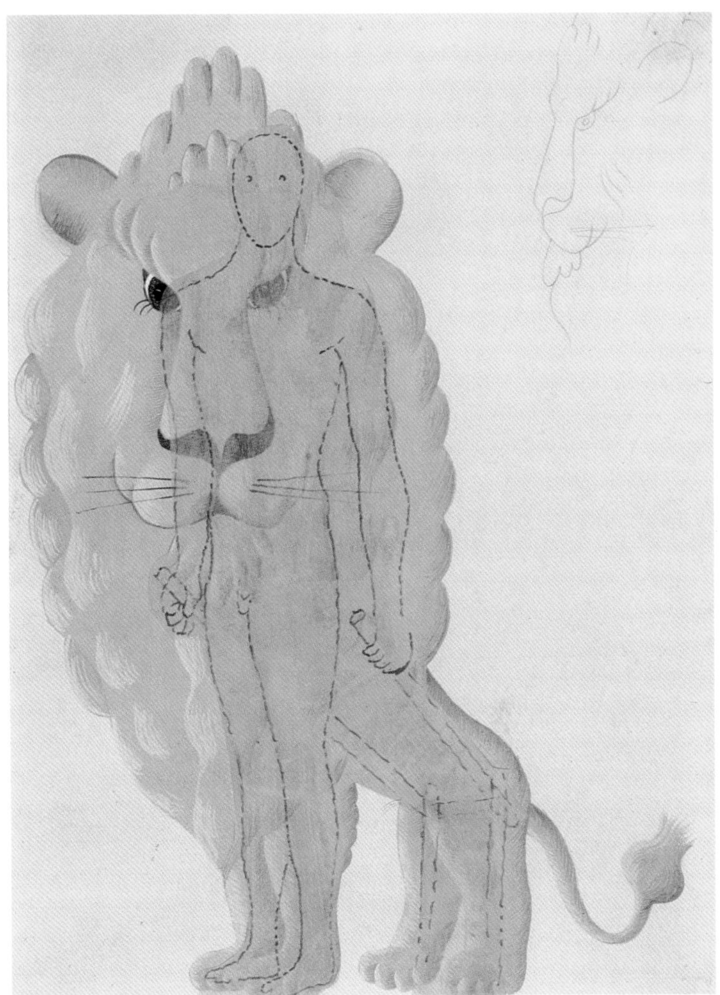

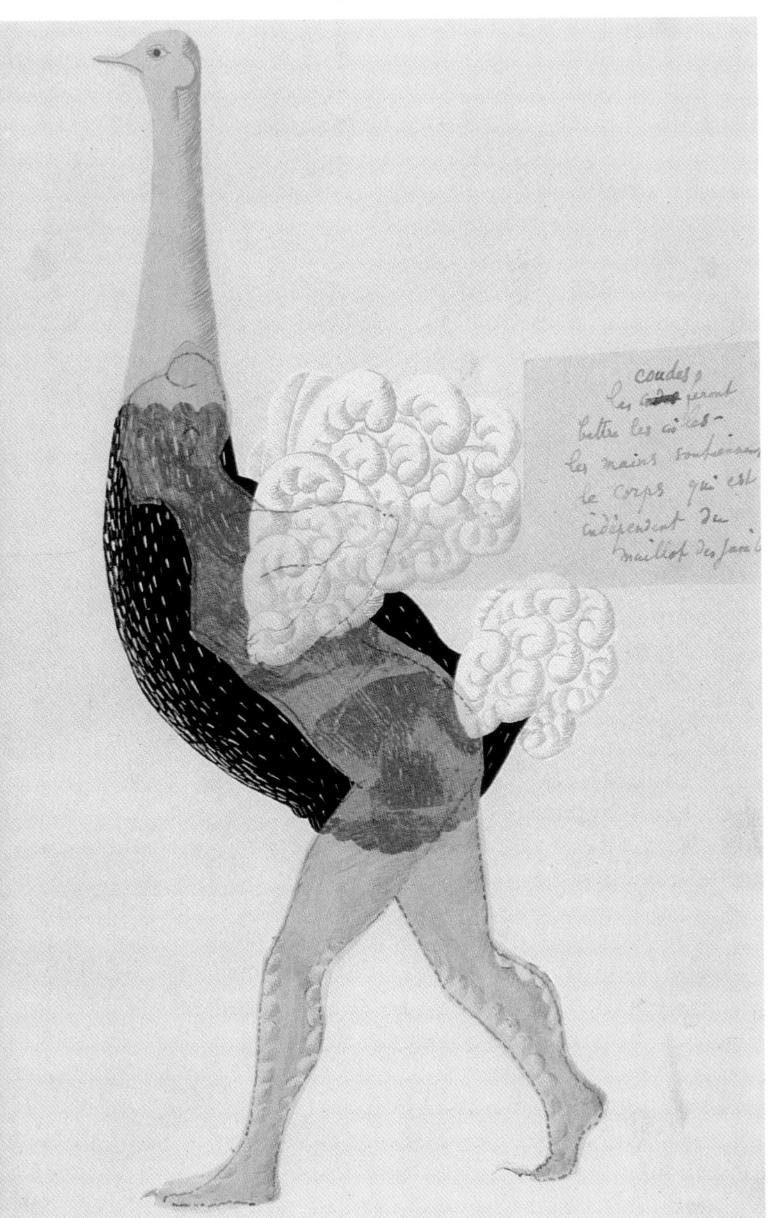

Fig. 20
JEAN HUGO
Costume design for the Lion in *Les Mariés de la Tour Eiffel*, 1921, cat. no. 46.

Fig. 21
JEAN HUGO
Costume design for the Ostrich in *Les Mariés de la Tour Eiffel*, 1921, cat. no. 45.

Fig. 22
FERNAND LÉGER
Set design for *Skating Rink*, 1921, cat. no. 61.

Fig. 30
Inger Friis and Jean Börlin in *Le Roseau*, 1924, cat. no. 234.

Swedes were "more bizarre than the Russians and heavier on their feet."[48] Together with the mixed reviews, headlines such as "Swedish Ballet Proves Orgy of Weird Impressionism" and "Swedish Ballet Seldom Dances" did little to help entice audiences, which were variously described as being "woefully small" and "of distressingly scant proportions" in most of the cities where the company performed.[49]

In addition to Gerald and Sara Murphy and Cole Porter, de Maré's artistic circle included several other Americans: the synchromist painters Morgan Russell and Stanton MacDonald-Wright, and the literary critic Edmund Wilson, who hoped to organize a Ballets Suédois production performed by Charlie Chaplin. (Although ideas were discussed, these potential collaborators were never directly involved in the realization of a ballet.) Because of the disappointments of the American tour, which included the cancellation of performances on the West Coast, de Maré abandoned his plans for the company to spend six months of each year in the United States and the other six in Paris.[50]

When the Ballets Suédois returned to France de Maré initiated legal proceedings against the American organizers of the tour, who had, among other things, postponed the original date of the troupe's premiere, failed to obtain a promised venue at the Metropolitan Opera, established unusually high ticket prices, and announced a two-week break in the middle of the run. De Maré dropped the case when he realized that, living in Paris and not being an American, he had little chance of winning. It was at this point that he quietly began selling works from his art collection to ensure the company's survival.[51]

The 1924–25 Paris season of the Ballets Suédois saw the premieres of five new ballets, one of which, *Relâche* (Cancelled), was both a triumph and an ending: it seemed that theatrical experimentation could go no further.

On the first program de Maré and Börlin once again presented a smorgasbord of productions, which included a sensuous evocation of Persia entitled *Le Roseau* (The Reed Player) (Figs. 28–30) and an Italian farce, *La Jarre* (The Jar). Based on a short story by Luigi Pirandello, with designs by Giorgio de Chirico and music by Alfredo Casella, *La Jarre* dramatized everyday life in a rustic Sicilian village (Figs. 31–32). Börlin traveled to Italy to refresh his knowledge of Italian folk dancing, which figured heavily in the production along with commedia dell'arte slapstick and pantomime. The ballet was performed in front of a stark architectural landscape, designed by de Chirico, and painted in opaque colors to echo those of his costumes (Figs. 33–34).

Also included on this program was *Le Porcher* (The Swineherd), a ballet based on Hans Christian Andersen's fairy tale of the same title, performed to a medley of Swedish folk music. This was followed by *Le Tournoi singulier* (The Singular Tournament), designed by Tsuguharu-Léonard Foujita, which reworked a classical myth of love and folly and set the action on a golf course (Fig. 35).

This program, which also included Léger's provocative spectacle *La Création du monde*, was in keeping with the Ballets Suédois formula of presenting works of thematic diversity and contrast, with contemporary as well as folkloric references, and featuring—above all—a strong pictorial emphasis.

A fortnight later Paris audiences would flock to the Théâtre des Champs-Elysées for the rescheduled premiere of the company's most iconoclastic production, *Relâche*, which can be variously translated as "cancelled," "relaxation," "break," and "letting go." The first perfor-

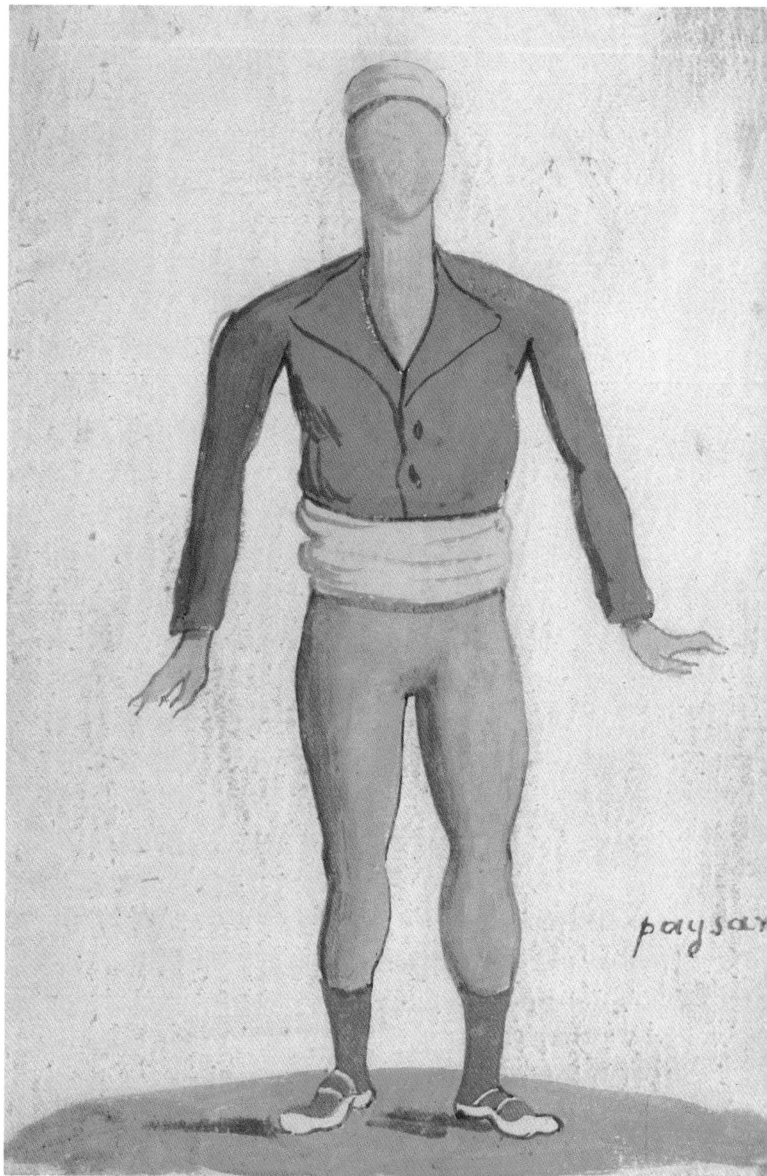

Fig. 31
GIORGIO DE CHIRICO
Costume design for a Young Lad in *La Jarre*, 1924, cat. no. 11.

Fig. 32
GIORGIO DE CHIRICO
Costume design for a Young Lad in *La Jarre*, 1924, cat. no. 11.

mance of *Relâche* was, ironically, delayed for one week because Börlin was temporarily ill.

The only two-act ballet in the repertory, *Relâche* was designed by the dada artist Francis Picabia, with music by Erik Satie and a filmed entr'acte by René Clair. Satie proposed Picabia as the designer and together they dominated all aspects of the production; the scenarios they created for *Relâche* and *Entr'acte* severely restricted the choreographic efforts of Börlin.[52]

In an interview with de Maré published in *Comoedia* on the day of the ballet's intended premiere, Picabia announced his frustration with the "pretentious absurdities" of the theater, stating that its cerebral possibilities had been exhausted and that with *Relâche* he was seeking a more visceral pleasure:

I want only a joy comparable to that of a beautiful night of love, comparable to the delight of lying in the sun, of doing 120 [km/hr] in an auto, comparable to the pleasure of boxing or to that of being stretched out on a mat in an opium den.[53]

For Picabia *Relâche* was also an expression of "contempt for yesterday, for the weight of the past which prevents today from shining."[54]

The scenario (see Plot Summaries, this volume) juxtaposed a series of seemingly unrelated actions. These included the appearance of a chain-smoking fireman who poured water from one bucket into another, a man in evening dress (dada artist and photographer Man Ray) who periodically rose from a chair to measure segments of the stage floor, a woman in a sequined gown (Edith Bonsdorff) who left her seat in the audience to smoke a cigarette onstage while the orchestra played, a man (Börlin) pedaling in a wheelchair tricycle, eight men in formal attire who joined the performers from the auditorium and proceeded to strip down to long underwear, and the arrival of the ballet's creators onstage in a Citroën motorcar.

This chaotic assemblage of activities took place in front of a dazzling backdrop made up of silver metallic disks, each with a light bulb in the center. Throughout the first act these lights periodically dimmed and brightened, sometimes blinding the audience. Act 2 incorporated a black curtain painted with white arrows, disks, targets, squiggly lines, the names of the ballet's creators, and rude comments such as "There are those who prefer the ballets of the Opéra. . . poor imbeciles." In concept and design, *Relâche* was a forerunner of much later trends, including the happenings and performance art of the 1960s and the graffiti art of today.

The backdrops and costumes, designed in black, white, gray, and silver, gave the ballet a cinematic character that integrated the production's two acts with the film *Entr'acte*, shown during the intermission. Although *Within the Quota* had reflected contemporary interest in the cinema, *Relâche* was the first ballet to actually incorporate film. As the filmmaker Clair related, "When I met [Picabia] he explained that he wanted to have a film projected between the two acts of the ballet, as was done before 1914 during the interval at café concerts."[55]

In an article entitled "Vive 'Relâche'," Léger praised the production, which he likened to a "game of the unexpected":

The airtight partition which separates ballet from the Music-Hall is broken. The actor, the dancer, the acrobat, the screen, the stage, all these means of creating a spectacle are grouped and organized. A single purpose brings a scene to life. All prejudices collapse.[56]

Léger also credited Börlin for contributing to the success of the ballet, describing him as

the first dancer who has understood the value of personal sacrifice for an ensemble. . . . He appears, disappears, in white, in black, metallic, dazzling, discreet and effaces himself to make way for equal talents.[57]

The article concludes in praise of de Maré:

Rolf de Maré [is] everywhere and nowhere—Bound to the stage, always ahead, always standing, tireless in pursuing novelty. Follow him. From "Les Mariés de la Tour Eiffel" to "Relâche," everthing is always advancing.[58]

Like many things new and challenging, the Ballets Suédois was difficult to sustain, and the end came suddenly. In early 1925 it was discovered that inadequate control at the Théâtre des Champs-Elysées box office had resulted in losses that aggravated the financial difficulties created by the American tour. De Maré would have had difficulty continuing to support the company out of his personal resources.

In addition, the partnership between de Maré and Börlin was also coming to an end. Börlin, having created twenty-three ballets in less than five years and given approximately nine hundred performances—dancing at least three leading roles on each program—was physically and creatively exhausted. Furthermore, de Maré had found a new lover, André Daven, whom he hired in an administrative capacity. Following a disappointing performance in Epernay, France, on 17 March 1925, de Maré announced his decision to disband the company.

Fig. 33
GIORGIO DE CHIRICO
Set design for *La Jarre*, 1924, cat. no. 9.

Fig. 34
La Jarre, Paris, 1924, cat. no. 236.

Fig. 35
TSUGUHARU-LEONARD FOUJITA
Set design for *Le Tournoi singulier*, 1924, cat. no. 28.

After five years of outstanding innovation the Ballets Suédois was almost entirely forgotten. The company's repertory was lost with Börlin's early death in 1930 at the age of thirty-seven. Except for a few pages of personal notation Börlin did not record his ballets, and there is virtually no film documentation.[59]

Dance scholarship has largely tended to ignore the company, treating it as a historic curiosity and a pallid imitator of the Ballets Russes. Among the reasons for this neglect are the troupe's multidisciplinary approach, which defied conventional categorization. In addition, the technical quality of the dancing was often uneven, and dance itself was frequently subordinated to the visual design.

Today our knowledge of the Ballets Suédois comes primarily through art—costume and set designs, drawings, paintings, photographs, posters, and sculpture. Börlin was indeed prophetic in envying the painters whose works have lived on to immortalize the company's extraordinary achievements.

1. Jean Börlin, "Pensées," quoted in *Cinquantenaire des Ballets Suédois 1920–1925: Collections du Musée de la Danse de Stockholm* (Paris: Musée d'Art Moderne de la Ville de Paris, 1971), 39.

2. Francis Picabia, "Rolf de Maré," *La Danse* (Nov.–Dec. 1924), unpaginated.

3. Birney P. Lynch, "It's Ebon Who Scores 'K.O.' in Ballet," *Syracuse Telegram*, 7 February 1924. The *Telegram* sent its sports editor to cover the Swedish Ballet's second performance at the suggestion of its dramatic editor, Chester B. Bahn, who wrote on 5 February 1924, following the company's first program, that the reviewing should have been done by a "specialist in things fistic."

4. Rolf de Maré, "Naissance et évolution des Ballets Suédois," *Les Ballets Suédois dans l'art contemporain* (Paris: Editions du Trianon, 1931), 20.

5. Michel Fokine, "Börlin, mon élève," *Les Ballets Suédois dans l'art contemporain*, 149.

6. De Maré, "Naissance," *Les Ballets Suédois dans l'art contemporain*, 25.

7. Tugal, "L'Art de Jean Borlin," *Les Ballets Suédois dans l'art contemporain*, 159.

8. Hans Alin, "The Swedish Ballet," *Scandinavia* (1923), 66–7.

9. Raymond Cogniat, *Décors de théâtre* (Paris: Chroniques du Jour, 1930), 13. Cited in Robley Munger Hood, "The Ballets Suédois: Modernism and the Painterly Stage" (Ph.D. diss., University of Denver, 1986), 64–5.

10. De Maré, "Naissance," *Les Ballets Suédois dans l'art contemporain*, 27.

11. Ibid.

12. "La Musique et la danse," *La Vie française*, 25 October 1920.

13. Nozière, "Propos de théâtre/Au théâtre des Champs-Elysées: Les Ballets Suédois," *L'Avenir*, 25 October 1920.

14. For a discussion of the Rubinstein/Nijinksa *Bolero* see Nancy Van Norman Baer, *Bronislava Nijinska: A Dancer's Legacy* (San Francisco: The Fine Arts Museums of San Francisco, 1986), 59.

15. Nozière, "Propos de théâtre," *L'Avenir*, 25 October 1920.

16. Jane Catulle-Mendes, "Les Ballets Suédois au Théâtre des Champs-Elysées," *Presse*, 24 October 1920.

17. "Le Ballet Suédois Has Exciting Experiences," *New York Post*, 9 December 1923.

18. *Derviches* was an expanded version of the solo *Derviche*, originally performed by Börlin at his debut concert in Paris on 25 March 1920.

19. Jean Bastia, "La Soirée," and Louis Laloy, "Les Ballets Suédois au Théâtre des Champs-Elysées: Iberia (Albéniz), Jeux (Debussy), Derviches (Glazounow), Nuit de Saint-Jean (Alfvén)," *Comoedia*, 25 October 1920.

20. "La Semaine théatrale et musicale," *Paris Midi*, 9 November 1920.

21. Ibid.

22. "Les Ballets Suédois vont donner leur troisième spectacle," *Bonsoir*, 19 November 1920.

23. "Théâtre des Champs-Elysées. Deuxième spectacles des 'Ballets Suédois,'" *Excelsior*, 10 November 1920.

24. "Les Ballets Suédois," *Bonsoir*, 19 November 1920.

25. De Maré, "Naissance," *Les Ballets Suédois dans l'art contemporain*, 28.

26. Bengt Häger, *Ballets Suédois*, trans. Ruth Sharman (New York: Harry N. Abrams, Inc. 1990), 26.

27. Tamara Nijinsky, *Romola and Nijinsky* (London: United Arts Publishers Ltd, 1991), 167.

28. SODRE: Archivo de la Teatro Solis, Montevideo, Uruguay. Nijinsky's last private performance took place on 19 January 1919 at the Hôtel Suvretta House in Saint-Moritz, Switzerland (Jean Pierre Pastori, *Soleil de nuit: La Renaissance des Ballets Russes* [Lausanne: Luce Wilquin Editrice], 100.)

29. Häger, *Ballets Suédois*, 28.

30. Antoine Banès, ibid.

31. Francis Steegmuller, *Cocteau: A Biography* (Boston: Little, Brown and Company, 1970), 267. *Les Mariés de la Tour Eiffel* had to change its first title, *La Noce massacrée*, at the request of Igor Stravinsky, whose ballet *Les Noces*, commissioned by Diaghilev, was in preparation. See Ornella Volta, "Svenska Baletten och de parisiska kompositörerna" (The Swedish Ballet and Parisian Composers), *Svenska Baletten i Paris, 1920–1925* (Stockholm: Dansmuseet, 1995), 69.

32. Lee Brown, "Now They're Saying It in Swedish," *Dance Lovers Magazine* (February 1924), 24.

33. Rosalie Housman, "New York Sees Novel Ballet," *San Francisco Call Examiner*, 12 December 1923. Of the group of musicians known as "Les Six," only Louis Durey failed to participate in this production. The score for *Les Mariés de la Tour Eiffel* was the sole composition to be produced collectively by the group.

34. Jean Cocteau to Jean Börlin after the premiere of *Les Mariés de la Tour Eiffel; Cinquantenaire des Ballets Suédois 1920–1925*, 54.

35. Jean Cocteau, "Les Ballets Suédois et les jeunes," *La Danse* (June 1921), unpaginated.

36. Fernand Léger, *Functions of Painting*, ed. Edward F. Fry, trans. Alexandra Anderson (New York: The Viking Press, 1973), 36.

37. André Levinson, *La Danse d'aujourd'hui: Etudes, Notes, Portraits* (Paris: Duchartte et Van Buggenhoudt, 1929), 393. Quoted in Melissa Ann McQuillan, "Painters and the Ballet, 1917–1926: An Aspect of the Relationship between Art and Theatre" (Ph.D. diss., New York University, 1979), 527.

38. Léger to de Maré, 21 November 1921, *Léger och Norden* (Léger and the North) (Stockholm: Moderna Museet, 1992), 27.

39. Léger to de Maré (n.d.), *Léger och Norden*, 30.

40. Léger to de Maré, 12 September 1922, *Léger och Norden*, 32.

41. Léger, *Functions of Painting*, 39.

42. Häger, *Ballets Suédois*, 43–5.

43. Brown, "Now They're Saying It in Swedish," *Dance Lovers Magazine*, 23.

44. Publicity leaflets in the collection of the Dansmuseet, Stockholm; and *Bethlehem [Pennsylvania] Globe*, 27 February 1924.

45. "More Exotic Beauty," *New York Evening Mail*, 27 December 1923.

46. "Ballet Unlike American Dance," *Harrisburg [Pennsylvania] Patriot*, 19 January 1924.

47. Leonard Liebling, "Swedish Ballet Proves Orgy of Weird Impressionism," *New York American*, 26 November 1923.

48. "Swedish Dancers," *Rochester [New York] Democrat*, 2 December 1923; "Success of Le Ballet Suédois Due to Young Dancers' Efforts," *New York American*, 11 November 1923.

49. Leibling, "Swedish Ballet Proves Orgy of Weird Impressionism," *New York American*, 26 November 1923; "Swedish Ballet Seldom Dances," *New York Evening Post*, 22 November 1923; "Scandinavians' New Dances Delight Garrick Audience," *New York Post*, 13 December 1923;

Chambers Hill, "O Yes; the Swedish Ballet," *Harrisburg (Pennsylvania) Telegram*, 19 January 1924.

50. Original plans for the 1923–24 American tour called for a six-week season in New York, to be followed by a tour of the country that would include performances on the West Coast. See "Swedish Ballet Coming This Fall," *New York Times*, 9 October 1923. According to Häger, *Ballets Suédois*, 47, de Maré hoped to establish a second base for his company in the United States, where he planned to spend six months of each year.

51. Häger, *Ballets Suédois*, 47.

52. "Relâche," *Les Ballets Suédois dans l'art contemporain*, 76.

53. De Maré, "A propos de 'Relâche,' Ballet instantanéiste," *Comoedia*, 27 November 1924.

54. Ibid.

55. René Clair, "Picabia, Satie and the First Night of 'Entr'acte,'" A Nous La Liberté *and* Entr'acte: *Films by René Clair*, trans. Richard Jacques and Nicola Hayden (London: 1970), 109. Quoted in McQuillan, "Painters and the Ballet," 653.

56. Léger, *7 arts Bruxelles*, 1 January 1925. Quoted in *Léger och Norden*, 45.

57. Ibid.

58. Ibid, 46.

59. *Derviches* was the only dance choreographed by Börlin to be filmed (see Häger, *Ballets Suédois*, 56). There is also a short documentary showing the company performing Swedish folk dances at the outdoor museum of Skansen, near Stockholm, on its 1922 tour. Given de Maré's interest in film, it's surprising that he never used the medium to record any Ballets Suédois productions. In an interview published in *Scenario* (1 March 1921), quoted in Häger, *Ballets Suédois*, 56, de Maré explained that "there is too big a gap between dance and screen. We are faced with a question of rhythm and timing which is difficult to sort out. It would require the reel to be run by an invisible conductor."

ANIMATING A VISION
ROLF DE MARÉ, JEAN BÖRLIN,
and the
FOUNDING OF THE BALLETS SUÉDOIS

Erik Näslund, Director, Dansmuseet, Stockholm

Swedish impresario Rolf de Maré and dancer-choreographer Jean Börlin were totally different in both personality and background. But their passion for art and dance joined them together, and the result found a place in dance history. Börlin could realize onstage the dreams of the art collector de Maré, while de Maré had the economic means to produce what Börlin in his turn dreamed of. The creation of both men, the Ballets Suédois came into being in Paris in autumn 1920.

The company lived for five intensive years, touring Europe and the United States, using the Théâtre des Champs-Elysées in Paris as its base. In the French press de Maré was described as "the Swedish Diaghilev," an apt comparison, because both men opened new paths for the art of dance by inviting the most exciting visual artists of the time to participate in their productions and both went to Paris to realize the ballet ensemble they envisioned. Serge Diaghilev's arrival there with his troupe of dancers from the Maryinsky Theater in St. Petersburg is well documented, but why de Maré and Börlin chose to launch their troupe in France and not Sweden is less well known.

Provincialism characterized the cultural life of Sweden during the first two decades of the century, in stark contrast to what was happening in Germany, Russia, and France, countries bubbling with new ideas and impulses. Art, music, and theater in Sweden were still dominated by the reawakened nationalism of the 1890s. Painters had discovered the Swedish landscape and composers drew inspiration from folk music. The attitude toward new music, in particular that of Arnold Schönberg, was negative, and it was not until the '20s and '30s that new music received a prominent, albeit still contested, place in the repertory. With the exception of August Strindberg's 1907–10 experiments in Stockholm, theater lacked experimental initiative.

The first manifestations of modernity in painting took place in 1909–10 with two exhibitions by young artists who had been students of Henri Matisse in Paris; among these artists were Nils Dardel, Isaac Grünewald, Sigrid Hjerten, and Einar Jolin. Criticism of the Swedish fauvists was severe. They were said to have committed treason against Swedish painting and indeed against all national values. Naivism, fauvism, cubism, and futurism began to be evident during the 1910s, having reached Sweden through various publications and exhibitions (Fig. 1). The young writer—and later Nobel Prize winner—Pär Lagerkvist was the first to discuss modernism within literature and painting. Following a journey to Paris, where he studied expressionism and cubism in French painting, he published the manifesto *Ordkonst och bildkonst* (World-art and Picture-art) in 1913. He wrote

Fernand Léger
Program cover (back) for the Ballets Suédois, 1923.

STOCKHOLM
PARIS

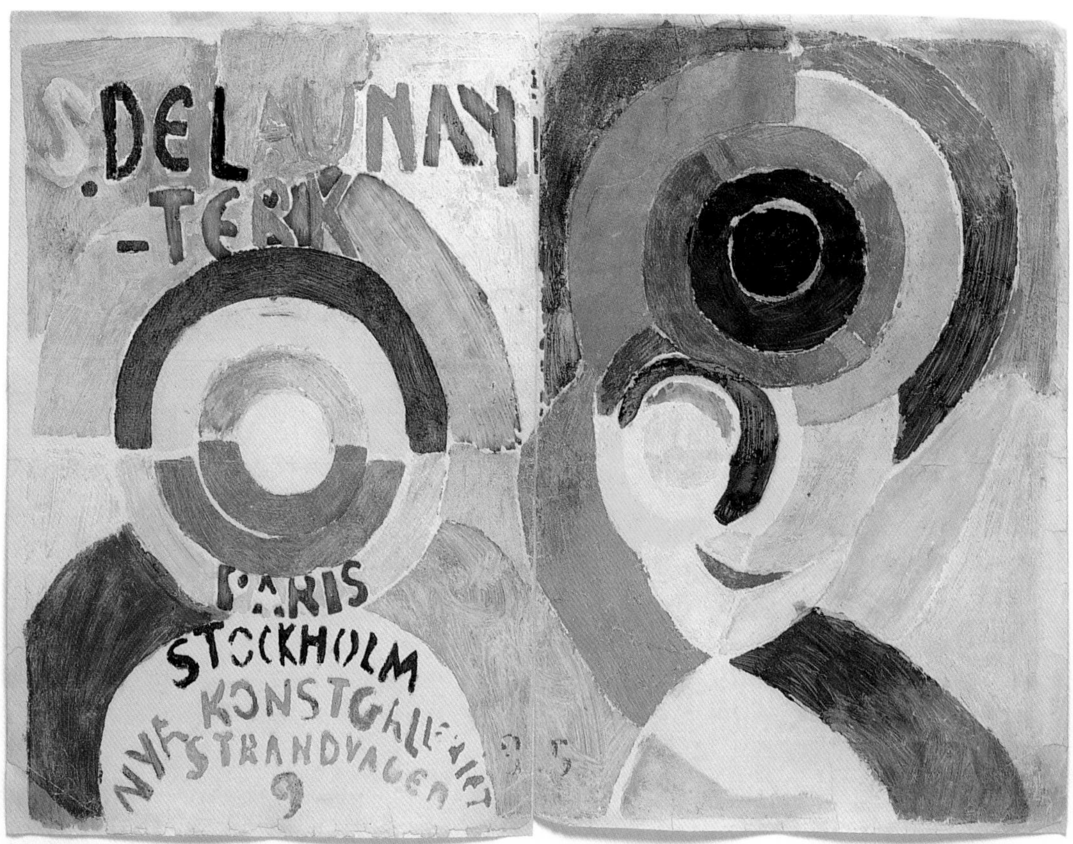

Fig. 1
SONIA DELAUNAY-TERK
(Gradizhsk, Ukraine 1885–1979 Paris, France)
Cover design for Stockholm exhibition catalogue with self-portrait and announcement of exhibition, 1916
Gouache and pochoir on paper, in two sections, 32 x 43 cm
Collection Martin Muller, San Francisco

in favor of total renewal, of an art uniting form and content into an inseparable whole that would be a true expression of the times. The words of Lagerkvist could be a suitable manifesto as well for the Ballets Suédois. De Maré came to know Lagerkvist through the painter Nils Dardel and on several occasions gave economic support to the young author. One of Lagerkvist's plays, *Himlens hemlighet* (Secret of the Heavens), was to provide inspiration for the ballet *Maison de fous* (Madhouse) (1920).

The development of dance in Sweden was stimulated by performances given by Isadora Duncan in Stockholm in 1906. She encouraged a young singer named Anna Behle to travel to her school outside Berlin and also to study with Emile Jaques-Dalcroze, a Swiss composer and teacher who developed the system known as eurhythmics. Behle would later return to Stockholm to open Sweden's first rhythmic institute in 1907. Anna Pavlova arrived in 1908 for her first appearances outside Russia, together with Adolf Bolm and a troupe of dancers from the Maryinsky Theater. They aroused enthusiasm with their classical repertory, including the second act of *Swan Lake* and *Paquita*. It was not until 1913 that Stockholm was to see a new Russian repertory, when Michel Fokine, who was to become important to Swedish ballet in general and the Ballets Suédois in particular, arrived for his first performance at the Royal Opera in Stockholm.

However, it was through painting that de Maré significantly came into contact with new artistic trends. His interest was fostered by his grandmother, Countess Wilhelmina von Hallwyl, heir to one of Sweden's greatest fortunes, who had in 1865 married the Swiss count Walther von Hallwyl. She was a passionate art collector, and in the 1890s the couple built a private palace in the center of Stockholm to house her extensive collection, a home that functioned as a museum. Ellen, one of the couple's three daughters, married Henrik de Maré, ultimately marshal of the court. Rolf de Maré was Ellen's only child. Ellen later fell in love with her son's private tutor and married him amid great scandal. When the count and countess broke off relations with their daughter, de Maré, then in his teens, moved into their palace where life was lonely and grave. He was further

Figs. 9–10
Rehearsal photographs:
Jean Börlin and the Ballets Suédios company,
Théâtre des Champs-Elysées, Paris, 1920, cat. nos. 180.

Fig. 11
Jean Börlin in his dressing room at the Théâtre des Champs-Elysées, Paris, 1920, cat. no. 179.

(Figs. 9–10). The company went to Paris in September where Dardel's young fiancée, Thora, who had arrived the year before, helped them settle. All the ballets would be tried out on stage with full decor and a ninety-piece orchestra led by the well-known Désiré-Emile Inghelbrecht. Meanwhile, massive advertising appeared in magazines owned by de Maré—*La Danse*, *Comoedia illustré*, *Paris Journal*, and *Le Monsieur*—although in the general press the Ballets Suédois would also prove to be newsworthy. De Maré assiduously gave interviews, as did Hébertot, whose press office was decorated in the Swedish national colors of blue and yellow. There he waved a small Swedish flag and spoke of his love for Sweden, but not for its journalists.

The 23 October *répétition générale* was a significant event and from then on the dress rehearsals of the Ballets Suédois would be great social occasions. The rehearsal was not attended by the Swedish minister, as an official expression of displeasure. The head of the Opera in Stockholm made it clear to the Paris correspondent of one of the Swedish daily papers that the Ballets Suédois was neither on tour from nor had anything in common with his institution.[15]

Critical praise, however, was to follow the Ballets Suédois for the next five years. Börlin, who was twenty-seven when the company made its debut, created twenty-four ballets, plus a number of solo compositions, and danced leading parts in practically all of them (Fig. 11). Besides choreographing, staging, and dancing, he held rehearsals and daily class. His accomplishment is even more remarkable since his experience as a choreographer was limited. Yet at the company's Paris premiere, Börlin presented four ballets, with an additional five the following month. The source of his creativity might be found in the travel and studies sponsored by de Maré.

In an interview in *Comoedia* in March 1920, Börlin told how he traveled to Switzerland and through France studying "popular rhythms" and dances, and then stopped in Milan before going to Spain. He studied Spanish dance in Granada, Madrid, and Seville—according to one source with José Otero, among others. Next he learned the art of the dervishes, apparently in North

Fig. 3
NILS SVENSSON
(Swedish, 18th century)
De favitska jungfruarna (The Foolish Virgins), late 1700s
Oil on canvas
Nordic Museum Archives, Stockholm

This eighteenth-century canvas inspired the costumes and decor for the Ballets Suédois production *Les Vierges folles* (1923). In this painting, the wise virgins are identified by their larger crowns and the bigger flames that they carry. The angel sounds a horn in their direction while disciplining the foolish virgins with a rod.

Fig. 5
Les Vierges folles, Paris, 1920, cat. no. 199.

works. De Maré entrusted Börlin with the difficult task of sequencing ballets on an evening's program. Because of their popularity with audiences, *Dansgille* and *Les Vierges folles* were often placed first or last. Sophisticated members of the audience, familiar with the classical tradition, experienced these Swedish ballets as exotica from the distant north.

On their tours of Europe and the United States the Ballets Suédois performed a selection of short pieces that included two folklore dances from Selinder's day, *Hallingen* and *Oxdansen*, which gave the male dancers the opportunity to show their power and technique as well as their sense of burlesque.

Swedish folk music was a natural element of these pieces. It also provided inspiration for *Le Porcher* (The Swineherd), a ballet based on Hans Christian Andersen's fairy tale of the same name. For this 1924 production the French composer Pierre-Octave Ferroud orchestrated a group of Swedish folk melodies.

Two other ballets used Swedish source material. The more unusual was *Maison de fous* (Madhouse), a dance-drama written by Jean Börlin that premiered during the first Paris season. With this production it was as if the tranquility of the classical ballet had been torn apart and replaced with expressions of intense anxiety based on an awareness of the terrors of modern warfare.

As Erik Näslund points out in this volume, there was a strong resemblance between *Maison de fous* and the Swedish author Pär Lagerkvist's one-act drama *Himlens hemlighet* (Secret of the Heavens), published in a collection of the writer's work in 1919.[6] In the same anxious spirit Dardel created an expressionist set for the ballet, with a terrifying symbol of human folly painted on the backdrop. The music was by the young Swedish modernist Viking Dahl, who was strongly influenced by his Russian contemporary Igor Stravinsky. As for the choreography, Carina Ari relates that Börlin encouraged the dancers to improvise movements and to work out the characterization of their roles individually.[7] In 1920 this was a new approach in the world of dance.

Audiences reacted strongly to *Maison de fous*, especially to the appearance and behavior of the lunatic Prince, danced by Börlin (Fig. 7), and the young girl's terrible fate—she is strangled by the man she loves. Following the ballet's premiere, a storm of controversy broke out: at the first performance the air was filled with whistling and booing as well as counteroffensives in the form of loud applause. Powerful reactions also appeared in the press; whenever it was performed the ballet would be greeted by vehement responses.

Finally there was *Offerlunden* (The Sacrificial Grove) in 1923, with music by the distinguished Swedish pianist Algot Johan Haquinius and sets and costumes by the Swedish painter Gunnar Hallström (Figs. 8–11). Börlin again drew upon Swedish history, this time going back to the Bronze Age.

The ballet tells the story of a king who sacrifices himself for the survival of the tribe. Such a sacrifice was depicted by the Swedish artist Carl Larsson (1855–1919) in his 1915 painting *Midvinterblot* (The Midwinter Sacrifice). In it people have gathered outside a pagan temple. Bronze horns are being blown and the naked king is awaiting the presiding priest's deadly blow. This is probably Sweden's most discussed and controversial work of art, and it provided Börlin with dramatic and pictorially stimulating material.

Hallström may well have been commissioned to work on *Offerlunden* because of his interest in antiquity. He supplied de Maré and Börlin with a large number of sketches, designing the sacrificial goblet, helmets, bronze horns, weapons, and jewelry with great historical accuracy. *Offerlunden* was not well received; it was performed only five times. Audiences as well as critics found the production overloaded with symbols and Wagnerian archaism.

Acknowledging the Swedish sources and elements of these five Ballets Suédois productions demonstrates how traditional Swedish culture was reinterpreted in the context of twentieth-century modernism.

1. Jean Börlin returned to Stockholm in 1923 to stage two productions from the Ballets Suédois repertory for the Royal Opera Ballet.

2. Rolf de Maré, *Les Ballets Suédois dans l'art contemporain*, (Paris: Editions du Trianon, 1931), 194.

3. Nils Dardel was not the first to depict the midsummer celebrations in Sweden. Among others to do so was Anders Zorn in his famous 1897 painting *Midsummer Dance*. Midsummer is still the main festival in Sweden.

4. *Les Ballets Suédois dans l'art contemporain*, 20.

5. Einar Nerman studied dance with Anna Behle in Stockholm from 1910 to 1915. Behle, a pupil of the Isadora Duncan school and Jaques Emile-Dalcroze, opened her school in 1907, the first of its kind in Sweden. From 1915 to 1919 Nerman toured Sweden, Norway, and England with various partners, creating both choreography and costumes. His later career was as a painter and stage designer.

6. Erik Näslund, *Carina Ari* (Stockholm: Interpublishing, 1984), 80.

7. Ibid.

Fig. 6
Carina Ari in *Dansgille*, Paris, 1921, cat. no. 214.

Fig. 7
Jean Börlin in *Maison de fous*, Paris, 1920, cat. no. 191.

Figs. 8–9
GUNNAR HALLSTRÖM
Costume designs for women in *Offerlunden*, 1923, cat. no. 35.

Fig. 10
Offerlunden, Paris, 1923, cat. no. 223.

Fig. 11
GUNNAR HALLSTRÖM
Costume design for a figure in white in *Offerlunden*, 1923, cat. no. 37.

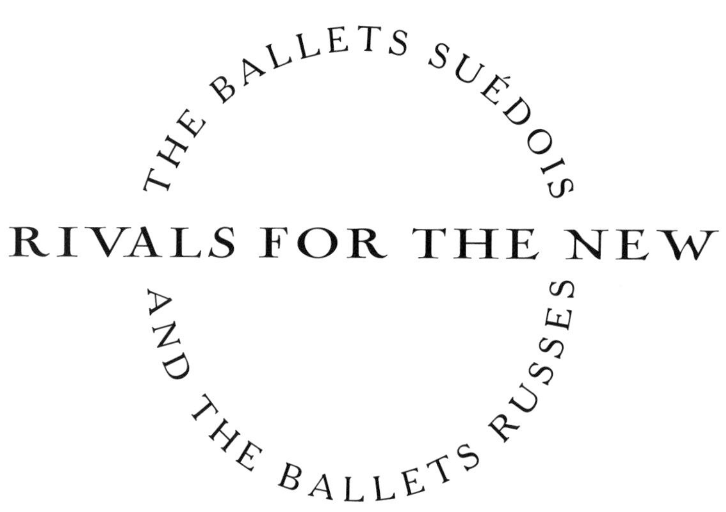

RIVALS FOR THE NEW: THE BALLETS SUÉDOIS AND THE BALLETS RUSSES

Lynn Garafola

In the early 1920s the Ballets Russes faced a rival that challenged its monopoly of avant-garde ballet—the Ballets Suédois. Organized by Rolf de Maré, the new company made its début at the Théâtre des Champs-Elysées on 25 October 1920 with an ambitious program of works choreographed by Jean Börlin, the company's star. Four ballets were given on the opening night—*Iberia*, *Jeux* (Games), *Derviches* (Dervishes), and *Nuit de Saint-Jean* (Saint John's Night, or Midsummer Night's Revel)—and in the course of the season, which lasted for nearly six weeks, five new ones were added—*Divertissement*, *Maison de fous* (Madhouse), *Le Tombeau de Couperin* (The Tomb of Couperin), *El Greco*, and *Les Vierges folles* (The Foolish Virgins). The premiere was a glamorous affair. Serge Diaghilev, anxious to weigh the potential threat to his own enterprise (then performing in London), braved a Channel crossing for a glimpse of the new company, which ended its season only days before his Ballets Russes was scheduled to open at the same theater.

Diaghilev had genuine cause for concern. The Ballets Russes had managed to survive the First World War, but financially its position was shaky. Rich Russian patrons had disappeared with the Revolution, German touring venues with the Axis defeat. For months the company had been a "turn" on the English music-hall stage, while its grand postwar comeback at the Paris Opéra early in 1920 had been marred by a two-week strike of Opéra personnel. And where the opening season of the Ballets Suédois would offer fifty-odd performances, the Ballets Russes season that followed would consist of fewer than a dozen.

Still, Diaghilev must have found some consolation in the identity—or lack of identity—of the rival enterprise. To all appearances the new company was a knock-off of the Ballets Russes, from its name, which meant "Swedish Ballet," to its repertory, roster of collaborators, and general aesthetic approach. Indeed, most of the works presented during the troupe's maiden season recalled its Russian predecessor. *Iberia*, for instance, drew on the Spanish idiom of *Le Tricorne* (1919); *El Greco* on the painterly approach of *Las Meninas* (1916); and *Nuit de Saint-Jean* on the stylized neoprimitivism of *Le Soleil de nuit* (1916). The eighteenth-century setting of *Le Tombeau de Couperin* (Fig. 1) was reminiscent of *Le Pavillon d'Armide* (1909), while the Chopin music and romantic style of *Divertissement* and *Pas de deux* invoked *Les Sylphides* (1909).[1] *Jeux*, premiered by the Ballets Russes in 1913 and now recreated by the Ballets Suédois, testified even more dramatically to de Maré's adoption

Fig. 2
PAUL COLIN
Jean Börlin, 1924, cat. no. 15.

PAUL
COLIN

of the Diaghilev recipe.

Not only did de Maré model his initial repertory on that of the Ballets Russes, he also enlisted a number of Diaghilev collaborators. These included the composers Claude Debussy (*Jeux* and *La Boîte à joujoux* [The Toy-Box]) and Maurice Ravel (*Le Tombeau de Couperin*), the painter Pierre Bonnard (who designed the scenery for *Jeux*), and the poet Jean Cocteau (who created *Les Mariés de la Tour Eiffel* [The Newlyweds on the Eiffel Tower]). De Maré also drew on key Diaghilev collaborative ideas. Rejecting the nineteenth-century specialist tradition, he commissioned stage designs from easel painters and scores from symphonic composers, free-lancers who formed the company's larger creative community. He viewed ballet as a fully collaborative medium where artists met as equals and performance combined the functions of art gallery, concert hall, and theatrical showcase. "Modern ballet," he wrote in 1926, "is... the synthetic fusion of four fundamentally divergent arts: choreography, painting, music, and literature.... The Swedish Ballet has always held as its principle the intimate association of the[se] four arts... [which] mutually supplement one another [and] offer the possible approach to a perfect totality."[2]

Finally, like Diaghilev before him, de Maré used the exotica of folklore to define the national character of his enterprise. Even if a number of dancers were actually Danish,[3] the display of traditional Swedish costumes, themes, and dances in works like *Nuit de Saint-Jean* and *Dansgille* (Dance Feast or Dances at a Gathering) certified the company's "native" identity. Nonetheless, like the Ballets Russes, the Ballets Suédois was preeminently a showcase for the modern. The company's scores (apart from the traditional music for its Swedish works) were either new or recently minted; its decors reflected current trends in painting and stage design; its choreography explored contemporary idioms and styles. The organization of the company also followed the lines of its predecessor. Privately financed, it was a vehicle for its male star, de Maré's protégé and lover Jean Börlin. If imitation is any measure of success, Diaghilev had good reason to be flattered by the new venture.

The Ballets Suédois had resources, however, of which Diaghilev could only dream. De Maré, a millionaire, poured a fortune into the company. The dancers wore costumes from the ateliers of Marie Muelle and Max Weldy, leading Paris costume houses, and dresses by the couturière Jeanne Lanvin. The sets were executed by Georges Mouveau, the Opéra's head scene painter. Guest conductors were sometimes brought in and, on occasion, soloists and even special orchestras: one hundred musicians were hired for the opening season alone. Posters were commissioned from Paul Colin (Fig. 2), Francis Picabia, and Miguel Covarrubias.

Fig. 1
Jean Börlin and Carina Ari in *Le Tombeau de Couperin*, Paris, 1920, cat. no. 193.

To ensure the proper environment for his enterprise de Maré took a seven-year lease on the Théâtre des Champs-Elysées, the magnificent art-nouveau theater where *Le Sacre du printemps* had received its premiere. He founded *La Danse*, the only Paris dance magazine of the period, which chronicled the activities of the company at length, while according the Ballets Russes only a fraction of the coverage. De Maré also acquired the publications *Le Monsieur*, *Paris-Journal*, and *Le Théâtre*. This last was a glossy monthly that merged with *Comoedia illustré* in 1922, eliminating another source of publicity for the Ballets Russes, whose programs for years had appeared as inserts in the semimonthly magazine.

The new company quickly struck out on its own. A publicity leaflet (Fig. 3) for its November 1921 season, which opened in Paris just weeks after the London premiere of Diaghilev's *The Sleeping Princess*, announced the change in direction in the provocative tones of a dada manifesto and in terms that cast the Ballets Russes as a reactionary bogeyman:

Les Ballets Suédois
donneront leur spectacle d'ouverture le 20 Novembre au
Théâtre des Champs-Élysées
Les Ballets Suédois
sont les seuls qui "OSENT"
Les Ballets Suédois
sont les seuls représentatifs de la vie contemporaine
Les Ballets Suédois
sont les seuls qui soient vraiment contre l'académisme.
CONTRE TOUS LES ACADÉMISMES
Les Ballets Suédois
sont les seuls qui puissent plaire au public international parce que Rolf de Maré ne pense qu'au plaisir de l'évolution.
Les Ballets Suédois
ne cherchent pas à être anciens, ne cherchent pas à être modernes; ils sont en dehors des absurdités que l'on nous montre sous prétexte d'ART THÉATRAL; ils vont propager la RÉVOLUTION par un mouvement d'où les conventions sont chaque jour détruites pour y être remplacées par l'invention.
VIVE LA VIE

Fig. 3
Publicity leaflet for the Ballets Suédois, 1921.

Only the Ballets Suédois "DARES."
Only the Ballets Suédois represents contemporary life.
Only the Ballets Suédois is truly against academicism.
AGAINST ALL ACADEMICISMS.
Only the Ballets Suédois can please an international public because Rolf de Maré thinks only about the pleasure of evolution. The Ballets Suédois seeks neither to be old nor to be modern; it stands beyond the absurdities mounted under the pretext of THEATRICAL ART; it propagates REVOLUTION by a movement that every day destroys convention by replacing it with invention.
LONG LIVE LIFE.[4]

Between 1921 and 1924 de Maré largely succeeded in edging Diaghilev to the sidelines of avant-garde Paris. Although the Ballets Russes produced a few works with impeccable avant-garde credentials, including Prokofiev's *Chout* and Stravinsky's *Le Renard*, it was only in 1923 that Diaghilev staged a modernist masterpiece that transcended the best of his rival's offerings. *Les Noces*, probably the greatest dance work of the decade, teamed three of his closest Russian collaborators: Stravinsky as composer, Natalia Goncharova as designer, and Bronislava Nijinska as choreographer. For the most part, however, the productions of these years reveal a Diaghilev more closely attuned to the conservative temper of the Right Bank than to the dadaist atmosphere of Montparnasse. From *Le Mariage d'Aurore* and *Le Spectre de la rose*, high points of the 1922 season, to *Les Tentations de la bergère*, *Cimarosina*, and the series of nineteenth-century operas—Emmanuel Chabrier's *Une Education manquée*, Charles Gounod's *La Colombe*, *Le Médecin malgré lui*, and

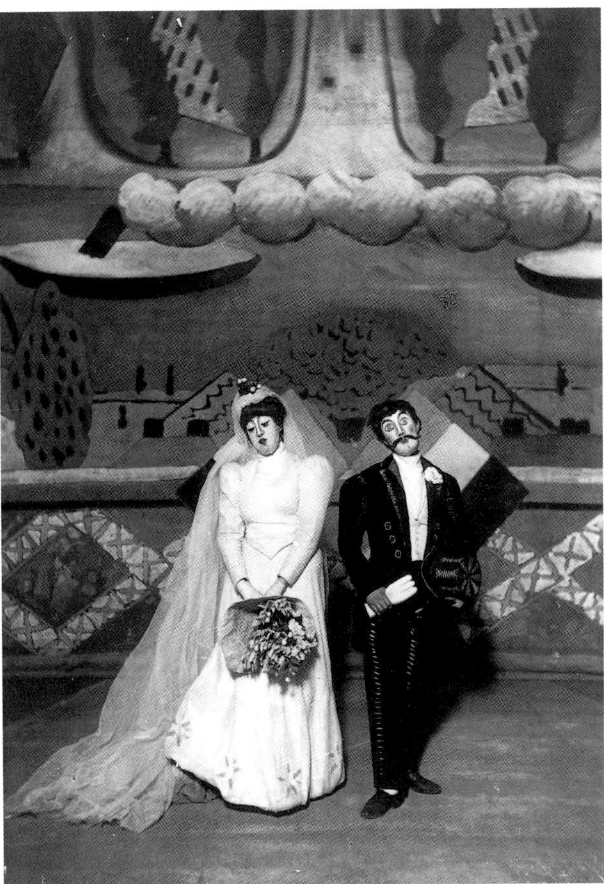

Fig. 4
Margit Wåhlander and Paul Eltorp in *Les Mariés de la Tour Eiffel*, Paris, 1921, cat. no. 210.

Philémon et Baucis—presented in Monte Carlo early in 1924, a significant part of the Ballets Russes repertory turned away from modernism and themes from contemporary life.

For the Ballets Suédois, by contrast, these were years of frenzied experiment, as the company became a meeting ground for the most exciting young talents of Paris. A key figure in this ferment was Jean Cocteau. An early enthusiast of the Ballets Russes, he had contributed to two of its productions, the lackluster *Le Dieu bleu* (1912) and *Parade* (1917), a small gem that evoked the poetry of the fairground and, through the designs by Picasso, brought cubism to the ballet stage. Three years later, at the Comédie des Champs-Elysées, Cocteau produced *Le Boeuf sur le toit*, an "American farce," as he described it, "by a Parisian who has never been in America," set in a Prohibition-era speakeasy.[5] The following year came *Les Mariés de la Tour Eiffel*, another tribute to the "poetry and miracle of everyday life," represented this time by a madcap wedding party at the most famous monument of Paris (Fig. 4).[6] The work grew out of Cocteau's Saturday-night dinners with the "faithful"—painters Jean Hugo, his wife, Valentine Gross Hugo, and Irène Lagut; writers Paul Morand and Raymond Radiguet; and the composers of the group recently baptized "Les Six"—Louis Durey, Georges Auric, Francis Poulenc, Germaine Tailleferre, Arthur Honegger, and Darius Milhaud. Nearly all contributed to *Mariés*: sets were by Lagut, costumes and masks by Jean Hugo, and music by all the members of Les Six except Durey; it was reviewed in *La Nouvelle Revue française* by Paul Morand.[7] Cocteau was temporarily at odds with Diaghilev and so offered the work to de Maré, who promptly offered him a contract.[8]

Along with *Mariés*, the outstanding work of the 1921 season was *L'Homme et son désir* (Man and His Desire). Conceived by Milhaud and the poet and dramatist Paul Claudel during his wartime diplomatic service in Brazil, the work was intended for Vaslav Nijinsky, whose appearance with the touring Ballets Russes had "so impressed" Claudel that he "immediately conceived the subject of a ballet for him."[9] However, Nijinsky's dancing days were numbered, and Diaghilev, whom Milhaud approached in 1920, rejected the project. "My symbolic and dramatic ballet," the composer wrote, "no longer corresponded with the needs of the day."[10] Milhaud took the work to de Maré, who agreed to stage it in spite of the expense of hiring the four singers, eleven instrumental soloists, and seventeen extra percussion instruments required by the score.

"A plastic drama. . . born of the Brazilian forest," as Claudel described the ballet in a program note, *L'Homme et son désir* was a work of major significance. The theme, he wrote elsewhere, is that of "man trapped in a passion, an idea, a desire, and vainly endeavouring to escape, as though from a prison with invisible bars, until the point when a woman, the image of both Death and Love, comes to claim him and take him with her offstage."[11] The score was equally provocative, with passages for unaccompanied percussion—clashing cymbals, tiny bells, panpipes—that evoked the nocturnal sounds of the forest, the ballet's primal world. The most striking aspect of the production was its setting, which Claudel had worked out with the painter Audrey Parr. The stage was divided into four tiers (including the stage floor) representing the different planes of symbolic action. On the uppermost tier were the Hours, a dozen women who moved across the stage for the entire duration of the action, framing it temporally and spatially. Just below was the flame-colored Moon, and on the lowest tier, her shadow; groups of musicians were ranged vertically at the sides.

The drama unfolded at the center: here, clad only in

Figs. 5–6
Jean Börlin in *L'Homme et son désir*, Paris, 1921, cat.nos. 205.

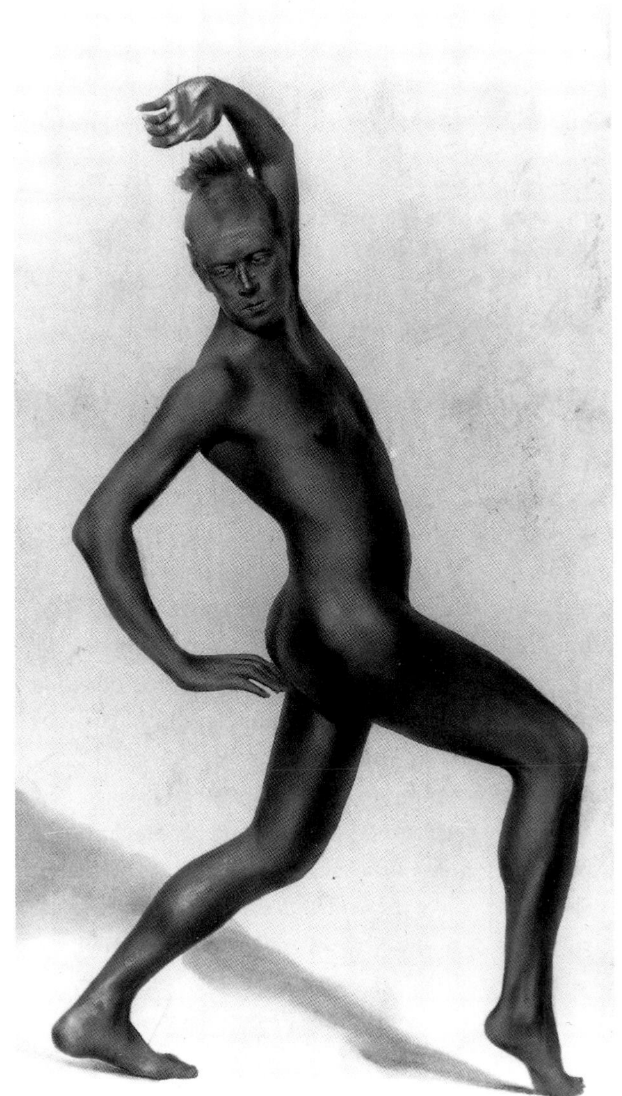

briefs and body makeup to create the effect of sculptural nudity, Man endured the torments of memory and illusion that ended only with the coming of day (Figs. 5–6). The mysticism that infused the work (critic Florence Gilliam spoke of "its trance-like remoteness" and "throb of hidden passion"),[12] along with the organization of stage space and the use of rhythmic movement, recalled Emile Jaques-Dalcroze's experiments at Hellerau, where Claudel's play *The Tidings Brought to Marie* had received its premiere in 1912.

In 1922 came another Ballets Suédois milestone, *Skating Rink*. The work was based on a prose poem by Ricciotto Canudo, who saw the rink as a mirror of contemporary life—anguished, full of carnal longing, hate, and desperation. From the incessant circling of the crowd to the frenzied lovemaking of the Madman to the sudden intrusion of his knife-wielding rival, the ballet pulsed with violence and working-class life in the raw. The score, by Honegger, was as feverish as the action, "speed[ing] along," as critic Emile Vuillermoz put it, "like the skaters' roller skates on the cement floor, . . . lit by the arc lamps and muffled by the cigarette smoke."[13]

As with *L'Homme et son désir*, the most striking aspect of the ballet was its design. The curtain, scenery, and costumes were by Fernand Léger, and their bold geometric shapes, flattened perspectives, and brilliant colors formed an enormous abstract painting. Léger conceived the action as an interplay of moving shapes and shifting color constellations, a sequence of images that changed according to the evolution of the dance but absorbed the dancer into the scenic landscape. "Léger does away with the dancer as a representation of human elements," wrote Maurice Raynal after the premiere. "The dancer, in his view, should become an integral part of the décor, a plastic element that will be a moving part of the décor's plastic elements." By way of example he describes a moment in the ballet where Léger arranged the "mobile decór"—or dancers—in contrasting masses, with "ten characters *in red, moving at speed* set against ten characters *in yellow, moving slowly*."[14] The approach was an extension of cubofuturist ideas that had circulated within the avant-garde since the early 1910s, and that Diaghilev had explored during the war, not only in *Feu d'artifice* (1917), which eliminated the dancer entirely, but also in Fortunato Depero's unrealized *Le Chant du rossignol*, where the artist described the chief interest of the dances as being the "movement of volumes."[15]

Léger's second commission for the Ballets Suédois was *La Création du monde* (The Creation of the World), produced in 1923. Probably the most distinguished of de Maré's productions, it teamed the painter with Milhaud and the poet Blaise Cendrars and drew on their common interest in African and African-derived folk forms. Based on African creation myths, the ballet owed its genesis to Cendrars, who had recently published an account of African folk beliefs under the title *Anthologie nègre*. The theme was timely. Although artists like Picasso and Henri Matisse had discovered African art long before the war, it was only in the immediate postwar years that it commanded widespread public attention. A number of events fueled this growing interest—Paul Guillaume's "Première exposition d'art nègre et d'art océanien" at the Galerie Devambez in May 1919; *La Fête nègre*, an evening of avant-garde performance organized by Cendrars and others at the Comédie des Champs-Elysées the following month;[16] and Börlin's *Sculpture nègre*, presented on a program of solo works at the same theater in March 1920. In addition, there was jazz. Introduced to Paris by American soldiers toward the end of the war, it invaded music halls and dance halls, concert halls and art galleries, prompting an exodus of African-American musical talent across the Atlantic.[17]

African-derived music had fascinated Milhaud ever since his days in Brazil. In 1922 he went to New York. The music he heard in Harlem was a revelation:

Against the beat of the drums the melodic lines crisscrossed in a breathless pattern of broken and twisted rhythms. A Negress whose grating voice seemed to come from the depths of the centuries. . . sang over and over again, to the point of exhaustion, the same refrain, to which the constantly changing melodic pattern of the orchestra wove a kaleidoscopic background. . . . Its effect on me was so overwhelming that I could not tear myself away.[18]

These Harlem memories found their way into *Création*. The orchestra of seventeen solo instruments was the same he had observed in Harlem, while the score made "wholesale use of the jazz style."[19] Critics dismissed the music as frivolous, or worse. "The feeling one gets listening to Darius Milhaud's latest production is rage," wrote Pierre de Lampommeraye in *Le Ménestrel*. "Going back to tom-toms, xylophones, bellowing brass, and noise is not progress."[20]

Léger, for his part, went far beyond his previous experiments. In *Création* the scenic elements themselves were mobile, while the human figure became a fully pictorial element indistinguishable from the surrounding objects. The curtain, in the style of synthetic cubism, rose to reveal three enormous deities, the gods of creation. Twenty-six feet tall, they were shifted by invisible dancers, and as they began to move, the creatures of a magical, African forest—birds, crocodiles, monkeys, insects—came to life. Finally, the first human couple was born. Masked and wearing black leotards tattooed in white, the two were joined by dancers enveloped in constructions that covered everything but their feet. Transformed into moving sculpture, the "human material," as Léger would later write, "had the same spectacle value as the object and the decor."[21]

Jazz in a lighter vein was featured in another work of the October 1923 season—*Within the Quota*. Conceived for the American tour that began the following month, the ballet teamed two expatriates, composer Cole Porter and painter Gerald Murphy, on this tale of immigrant-makes-good that opened in the United States just as Congress was about to severely restrict immigration. Diaghilev almost certainly missed the work in Paris, but had he seen it he would have found it detestable. "The whole of Venice," he wrote to Boris Kochno in 1926, "is up in arms against Cole Porter because of his jazz and his Negroes. He has started an idiotic night club on a boat . . . and now the Grand Canal is swarming with the very same Negroes who have made us all run away from London and Paris."[22] Although *Parade* had introduced both ragtime and the American theme to the ballet stage, Diaghilev dropped them both once they became associated with blacks. De Maré, by contrast, had an abiding interest in the cultural expressions of Africa and the African diaspora.[23] He made documentary films of African dance (which Börlin used in preparing *La Création du monde*) and, after the demise of the Ballets Suédois, presented both Josephine Baker (in *La Revue nègre*) and Florence Mills (in *Black Birds of 1926*) at the Théâtre des Champs-Elysées.

Relâche (Cancelled), the company's swan song, fully belonged to the Paris avant-garde. Conceived by Francis Picabia, a painter close to dada and the emerging group of surrealists, this "snapshot ballet in two acts with a cinematographic entr'acte" was practically a who's who of the international avant-garde. The music, based on children's round games, was by Erik Satie; the set, made up of 370 lights that dimmed and brightened with the music, was by Picabia; the film was directed by René Clair and featured cameo appearances by Man Ray, Marcel Duchamp, Satie, Börlin, Picabia, de Maré, and various other artists. "*Relâche* is life, life as I love it," wrote Picabia:

life without morrow, life today. . . . Automobile headlights, ropes of pearls, . . . advertising, music; men in evening dress; movement, play, clear and transparent water, the pleasure of laughter. . . . Relâche *strolls through life with a great burst of laughter.* Relâche *is aimless movement. Why think?*[24]

Why, indeed? As described by de Maré, the action was certainly bizarre:

[T]he curtain rose on a glittering and strange decor. . . . There were flashing floodlights that blinded the audience; a fireman who strolled about, smoking nonstop; a woman in an evening dress who made her entrance through the hall,. . . eight men in dinner jackets; games for the woman and several jumping jacks that went on until one of the latter carried her off.[25]

In the second act, the authors "trained a cannon at the audience"—posters with such provocative lines as: "Those who are discontent are authorized to clear out" or "There are some—poor imbeciles—who prefer the ballets at the Opéra."[26] Judging from the reviews, most of the critics fell into this category.

The Ballets Suédois cut a wide swathe through avant-garde Paris. Not only did the themes of ballets like *La Création du monde* reflect the interests and pastimes of its artists, but they were expressed in forms that linked the company to experiments on the artistic fringe: Léger's treatment of the performer as an "object-spectacle," for instance, recalls Georges Valmier's designs for the Théâtre Art et Action.[27] The company's visual artists received wide coverage in the avant-garde press, including expatriate journals like *transition* and *The Little Review*, which reproduced numerous works by Picabia and Léger. In September 1923 *L'Horizon*, a monthly devoted to the art of "today and tomorrow," published Cendrars's scenario for *Création*, an excerpt from Milhaud's score, and fifteen of Léger's designs.[28]

Although de Maré never formally identified the Ballets Suédois with either dada or surrealism, the network of artists that formed the company's larger community linked the enterprise to both movements. At the center of this network was Nils Dardel, a Swedish painter who had settled in Paris in 1910. A close friend of de Maré, Dardel had assisted him in assembling the vast collection of modern art that presaged his later commissions as an impresario. He also introduced de Maré to friends like Cocteau (whose Saturday night dinners Dardel regularly attended), Léger, Satie, and the composers of Les Six, as well as to the larger Left Bank community, in whose social doings Börlin sometimes participated.[29] Although ballet held only minimal interest for this community, it did turn out for certain Suédois events. Thus, in October 1923, at the invitation-only gala where Marcel L'Herbier filmed the riot scene of *L'Inhumaine* (a riot actually provoked by the

Figs. 7–8
Jean Börlin in the Royal Opera Ballet production of *Schéhérazade*, Stockholm, 1919, cat. no. 176.

music of George Antheil, making his Paris debut as a composer), the audience included Picasso, Satie, Man Ray, Ezra Pound, James Joyce, Constantin Brancusi, Milhaud (who wrote the film score), and various surrealists.[30] Left Bank artists also participated in a New Year's Eve revue by Picabia and René Clair that included the last performance of *Relâche*, a sex farce called *Ciné Sketch* (with Man Ray as the Blabbermouth, Duchamp as the Naked Man, and Börlin as the Constable), dances by Caryathis (*La Belle excentrique*, to Satie; *Le Jongleur*, to Poulenc; *Aujourd'hui*, to Auric), recitations by Yvonne George (the star of Cocteau's *Antigone*), and music by the Georgians, "the latest Jazz-band from New York.[31]

Although Diaghilev had little sympathy for the more extreme experiments of the Ballets Suédois, he was certainly not immune to its influence. Beginning in 1923 a number of artists associated with the Ballets Suédois received their first commissions from him. This group included not only Auric, Poulenc, and Milhaud, but also Giorgio de Chirico (who designed *La Jarre* [The Jar] in 1924 for de Maré and *Le Bal* in 1929 for Diaghilev), Henri Sauguet (who presented a short program of symphonic works at a Suédois performance in 1923 and in 1927 wrote the music for Diaghilev's *La Chatte*), and Man Ray (whose photographs would figure in Diaghilev programs). In addition to raiding de Maré's stable of artists, Diaghilev also dipped into his stock of ideas. Although *Parade* had drawn on contemporary material as early as 1917, seven years elapsed before the settings and activities of the modern world reappeared in his repertory. When they did, they nearly always bore the stamp of de Maré's "discoveries": *Les Biches* (1924) was composed by Poulenc; *Le Train bleu* (1924), by Milhaud; *La Pastorale* (1926), by Auric; and *La Chatte* (1927), by Sauguet. *Romeo and Juliet* (1926) had designs by Max Ernst and Joan Miró, surrealists whom Diaghilev stum-

Wilson called "the droll and homely aspects of the Parisian world."[52] The work's few dances all derived from this world of familiar pastimes—the polka for the Trouville bathing beauty (a role that Börlin himself sometimes danced), the quadrille and wedding march for the guests, and the two-step for the "telegrams," who looked like Tiller girls.

Skating Rink, too, drew on vernacular idioms—the gliding and endless circling of roller skaters and the rough, sexually-charged dancing of working-class *apaches*. In *Le Tournoi singulier* (The Singular Tournament), Eros carried a golf club and Folly danced a blues (Fig. 19), while in *Within the Quota*, Everybody's Sweetheart did a shimmy. André Levinson, who seldom had a good word for the company, criticized the dancing in this last work unmercifully. The Swedes, he wrote,

> *are as awkward on the dance floor as they are in a classical* ballabile. . . . *I consider it the maddest audacity on the part of the "Swedes" to pit themselves against performers of the music hall, those consummate virtuosi, flawless technicians, imbued with age-old traditions. . . who spend ten years elaborating and completing a turn. You want to make* Within the Quota *. . . a world success? Cast Nina Payne as the Jazz Baby, [Vicente] Escudero as the cowboy, Mr.[Louis] Douglas or John as the Negro, the Catalans as the Immigrant & the Fairy . . . . Here, then, is a superb theatrical theme—the ironic and picturesque apotheosis of Americanism—reduced to a trifle. Once all aesthetic controversy is put aside, the truth hits you: whatever the contribution of its painters, musicians, and poets, the Ballets Suédois will never succeed in creating a work of art so long as its ballets are danced by the Ballets Suédois.*[53]

Fig. 18
Jean Börlin in *Sculpture nègre*, Paris, 1920, cat. no. 182.

Although this criticism of the dancers in general and Börlin in particular seems unduly harsh, there were other complaints even during the earliest seasons, which Levinson never saw. Referring to the "manifestos" that accompanied the appearance of the company, Reynaldo Hahn wrote in 1920, "To declare that [Börlin's] young company is 'all of the highest order,' when a majority of its members would cut a sorry figure at the dance examinations of the Paris Opéra. . . is carrying panegyric. . . too far."[54] W. J. Turner, who reviewed the company in London just after its debut, echoed Hahn's criticism, although his tone was milder. In *Divertissement*, he wrote, the dancers "were somewhat heavy and rather below the standard to which the best of the Russians have accustomed us." Although P. J. S. Richardson, editor of *The Dancing Times*, had nothing but praise for Jenny Hasselquist, he felt that the technique of the company i n general "would doubtless be improved had they the advantage of daily tuition from a thoroughly experienced *maître de ballet*." Of the company's star he wrote: "M. Börlin suffers by failing to have that ballon and elevation which are so essential for the successful male dancer. As a mime he is remarkable."[55]

By 1923 even Florence Gilliam, who had strongly praised Börlin's performance in *L'Homme et son désir*, acknowledged his limitations. "As a dancer he has no great versatility. Certain pleasing attitudes, a graceful sense of movement, and a few interesting steps are his only equipment."[56] In another article published that year she singled out Kaj Smith as being a "more brilliant and . . . more varied dancer," noting that "Börlin's dance-steps are almost entirely restricted to certain attitudes

Fig. 19
TSUGUHARU-LÉONARD FOUJITA
Costume design for Folly in *Le Tournoi singulier*, 1924, cat. no. 29.

and turns which he employs indefatigably in ballets of the most diverse character," a point also made by Levinson.[57] Nevertheless she regarded Börlin as a choreographer who was "sophisticated," "gifted with imagination," and "intellectually advanced."[58]

Gilliam wrote this before the company embarked on the most experimental chapter of its history. Indeed the works she cites again and again are those mining the expressive vein opened by his exposure to modern German dancemaking. By contrast, she had no sympathy for the "monstrous inanities" of *Les Mariés de la Tour Eiffel*,[59] and one can only assume that she would have equally disliked its descendants—*Within the Quota*, *Le Tournoi singulier*, and *Relâche*—not only because of their self-conscious modernity, but also because of their designs, which overwhelmed the dancing and reduced it to inconsequence. With time Börlin himself grew resentful of this imbalance, telling Roland-Manuel, who composed the music for *Le Tournoi singulier*, that "the dancer must cease to be the sandwich man condemned to carry the great painters' advertisement boards."[60] Börlin's earliest works had eschewed design completely. Even in ballets like *Maison de fous*, *El Greco*, and *L'Homme et son désir* that incorporated visual elements, the design had supported rather than undermined the dance conception. De Maré's growing interest in artists like Picabia and Léger not only destroyed this balance but also threatened to evict dance entirely from the avant-garde performance gallery that the company had become.

De Maré later claimed that he had dissolved the Ballets Suédois because after *Relâche* it was possible neither to move ahead nor to turn back: "*Relâche*," he wrote, "was contrary to our Nordic spirit."[61] More to the point, he could not go forward without transforming the Ballets Suédois into an enterprise with no role for the choreographer it was intended to serve. And because de Maré had no genuine interest in ballet and had already lost millions, there was no compelling reason for him to turn back.

Compared to the Ballets Russes, the long-term contribution of the Ballets Suédois to twentieth-century dance has been slight. The reason for this has less to do with Levinson's "persistent scorn" for the company, as Bengt Häger insists,[62] than with de Maré's persistent deemphasis of its dance legacy. Ballets only survive as living entities when they are performed. After dissolving the Ballets Suédois, de Maré made no attempt to revive its works. Börlin, for his part, lacked both the means and the company to do so. Abandoned by his erstwhile mentor, Börlin tried his hand at acting, while continuing to give dance recitals both in France and abroad. With his death in 1930 the possibility of reviving any of his works vanished.

What survived of those works—designs, posters, programs, curtains, letters, photographs, press clippings—was squirreled away in a remarkable collection, all the more valuable because it remained intact. De Maré, who owned the collection, housed it initially at the Archives Internationales de la Danse, which he founded in Paris in 1932, later transferring it to the Dansmuseet in Stockholm, which he opened in 1953. Drawing on these materials he organized a few exhibitions. He also published *Les Ballets Suédois dans l'art contemporain* (1931), a limited-edition volume with more than sixty pages of photographs, fourteen color plates of designs, descriptions of the ballets (omitting the classical ones and the dances performed as divertissements), and dozens of published and unpublished statements by painters, writers, composers, and critics attesting to the importance of the company and its works. Only one dance artist—Fokine—was deemed worthy of inclusion. Although the volume was intended as a tribute to and vindication of Börlin, his contribution was outweighed by the emphasis placed on that of his prestigious collaborators. If the Ballets Suédois has been written out of dance history, it is because from early on dance was written out of the company's history by de Maré himself. For all that Börlin was the troupe's initial raison d'être, his legacy exists only to the extent of its presence in the company's "collectibles." In these autographed letters and libretti, signed posters, scores, photographs, and designs lies the true story of the Ballets Suédois. Among them the dancers, invisible, flit like ghosts in search of a past willed to oblivion.

1. Although Bengt Häger alludes to *Divertissement* in *Ballets Suédois*, trans. Ruth Sharman (New York: Abrams, 1990), 19, he does not list the work among the company's productions, nor is it mentioned in Rolf de Maré's *Les Ballets Suédois dans l'art contemporain* (Paris: Editions du Trianon, 1931) or the catalogue *Cinquantenaire des Ballets Suédois 1920–1925: Collections du Musée de la Danse de Stockholm* (Paris: Musee d'Art Moderne de la Ville de Paris, 1971). *Chopin*, a pas de deux (sometimes listed simply as *Pas de deux*), was another "classical" work mentioned by critics in reviews of the company's earliest seasons, but ignored in these publications. An undated program for the November 1921 season at the Théâtre des Champs-Elysées includes a *Chopin*, but since this was an ensemble work closely modeled on *Les Sylphides* (according to the program, it consisted of a "Valse," "Prélude," "Mazurka," "Etude," and "Valse brillante"), it was probably *Divertissement* under another name. The reason for the change in title may well have been the addition to the repertory in 1922 of *Divertissements* (or *Divertissement*), a potpourri of dances, including several solos, that recalls Anna Pavlova's programming. The individual items listed on programs for the 1922–23 American tour are *Greek Dance* (Grieg), *Siamese Dance* (Jaap Kool), *War Dance* (Berlioz), *Humoresque* (Florent Schmitt), *Valse—"Dame Kobold"* (Weingartner), *Dance of the Mountain Girl* (Alfven), *Anitra's Dance* (Grieg), *Dervish* (Glazunov), *Spanish Dance* (Rubinstein), *Arabic Dance* (Grieg), *Gypsy Dance* (Saint-Saens), *Halligen*, *Swedish Dance*, and *Oxdance*. None of these dances are listed in the major Ballets Suédois source books.

2. Rolf de Maré, "The Swedish Ballet and the Modern Aesthetic," trans. Kenneth Burke, *Little Review*, Winter 1926, 24. This article appeared in the magazine's special theater issue.

3. Rolf de Maré, "Les Ballets Suédois expression d'une époque," *Les Ballets Suédois dans l'art contemporain*, 27.

4. Reproduced in Häger, *Ballets Suédois*, 27.

5. Quoted in Erik Aschengreen, *Jean Cocteau and the Dance*, trans. Patricia McAndrew and Per Avsum (Copenhagen: Gyldendal, 1986), 89.

6. Ibid., 99.

7. Paul Morand, "Ballets Suédois: Les Mariés de la Tour Eiffel," *La Nouvelle Revue française*, 17, no. 95 (August 1921), 225.

8. For a reminiscence of the group and its activities, see chapters 3 ("Les dîners du samedi") and 5 ("Les mariés de la Tour Eiffel") of Jean Hugo's *Avant d'oublier 1918–1931* (Paris: Fayard, 1976).

9. Darius Milhaud, *Notes without Music* (New York, 1953; rpt. New York: DaCapo, 1970), 79.

10. Ibid., 109.

11. Quoted in de Maré, *Les Ballets Suédois*, 52. The English translation comes from Häger, 125.

12. Florence Gilliam, "Parade," *Gargoyle*, August 1921, 5.

13. Quoted in Häger, *Ballets Suedois*, 36.

14. Quoted ibid., 166.

15. Quoted in Melissa McQuillan, "Painters and the Ballet, 1917–1926: An Aspect of the Relationship Between Art and Theatre," (Ph.D. diss., New York University, 1979), 394.

16. The centerpiece of this performance was Cendrars's *La Légende de la création*, "transposed" by the poet from "Fang tradition." Although the piece included spoken and musical sections, it chiefly consisted of dances ("Danse de la reconnaissance des créatures," "Danse guerrière de Bétsi," "Danse de la provocation à la divinité," "Danse de l'arbre," "Danse totémiste des Mpongwés," "Danse de l'accouplement"), which were performed by Caryathis, Marcel Herrand, Djemil-Anik, Collin (or Colin) d'Arbois, Stasia Napierkowska, and "Mademoiselles" Redstone and Israel. According to Jean

Mollet, Djemil-Anik, who was from Martinique, appeared "completely nude, painted from head to toe by [Kees] van Dongen," while the other dancers wore costumes with "bunches of bananas" *(Les Mémoires du Baron Mollet* [Paris: Gallimard, 1963], 134). Three of the numbers, which were performed on "authentic native instruments," were adapted by Honegger. The costumes were designed and executed by Janine Aghion and the painter Guy-Pierre Fauconnet; the tattoos were by van Dongen, and the "ceremonial" was "arranged" by the painter André Dunoyer de Ségonzac and Luc-Albert Moreau. André Salmon referred to the impact of the event in an article published in *The Burlington Magazine:* "An exhibition of negro art held in a Parisian gallery at the beginning of last winter served to render familiar to the public, and to some extent popular, the interest of modern artists in the productions of African and Oceanic sculptors . . . . A fête nègre, as delightful as a charming Russian ballet, which was held on the occasion of this exhibition, seems to have greatly favoured the fashion but to have been of little service to the pure idea. And so although many amateurs of negro art. . . will have taken the trouble to revisit the incomparable collection at the British Museum, we cannot feel sure that each of them will see it with. . .eyes completely purified from a love of the curious and picturesque" (André Salmon, "Negro Art," *The Burlington Magazine,* 15 April 1920, 164).

17. For a summary of avant-garde events on African themes, see Laura Rosenstock, "Léger: 'The Creation of the World,'" in *"Primitivism" in 20th Century Art: Affinity of the Tribal and the Modern,* ed. William Rubin (New York: The Museum of Modern Art, 1984), 2:473–4.

18. Milhaud, 136–7.

19. Ibid., 149.

20. Quoted in Häger, *Ballets Suédois,* 44.

21. "The Spectacle: Light, Color, Moving Image, Object-Spectacle," in Fernand Léger, *Functions of Painting,* ed. and intro. Edward F. Fry (London: Thames and Hudson, 1973), 38.

22. Quoted in Boris Kochno, *Diaghilev and the Ballets Russes,* trans. Adrienne Foulke (New York: Harper and Row, 1970), 222.

23. Richard Brender, "Reinventing Africa in Their Own Image: The Ballets Suédois' 'Ballet nègre,' *La Création du monde,*" *Dance Chronicle,* 9, no. 1 (1986), 125. Brender situates the work and treatments of the African theme generally within the larger context of French colonialism.

24. Quoted in de Maré, *Les Ballets Suédois,* 75–6.

25. Ibid., 77.

26. Ibid., 78.

27. For Valmier, see Laurence Marceillac, "Cubisme et théâtre: Les Réalisations de Valmier pour Art et Action," *Revue de la société d'histoire du théâtre,* 35, no. 3 (1983), 338–46.

28. "Le Théâtre de demain. Les Ballets Suédois de Rolf de Maré. La Création du monde, ballet nègre," *L'Horizon,* September 1923, 1–2.

29. In Billy Klüver and Julie Martin, *Paris: Artists and Lovers 1900–1930* (New York: Abrams, 1989) two photographs (130–1) show Börlin surrounded by artists at costume balls organized by the Maison Watteau, a center for Scandinavian artists whose annual gatherings were "attended by everyone in Montparnasse" (95). Among the artists identified by the authors are Moïse Kisling, Tristan Tzara, Tsuguharu-Léonard Foujita (who designed *Le Tournoi singulier* for the Ballets Suédois in 1924), Marie Vassilieff, Per Krohg, and Dardel. It is unclear how fluent Börlin was in French. According to conductor D.-E. Inghelbrecht, who worked closely with him from 1920 to 1923, composed the score of *El Greco,* and eventually married the ballerina Carina Ari, Börlin "understood and spoke little French" *(Mouvement contraire: souvenirs d'un musicien* [Paris: Editions Domat, 1947], 130.)

30. George Antheil, *Bad Boy of Music* (Garden City, N.Y.: Doubleday, Doran, 1945), 134; "Courrier des théâtres," *Figaro,* 2 October 1923, 6; Klüver and Martin, *Kiki's Paris,* 134.

31. The program for this one-time-only event is in *MGZB (Ballets Suédois), Dance Collection, New York Public Library. A photograph by Man Ray showing Duchamp with a strategically placed handful of leaves appears in Klüver and Martin, *Kiki's Paris,* 137.

32. De Maré, *Les Ballets Suédois,* 23.

33. Léger, "The Spectacle," 39.

34. Erik Näslund, "Carina Ari," *Dance Research,* 7, no. 2 (Autumn 1989), 75–6.

35. Quoted in *Cinquantenaire des Ballets Suédois,* 39.

36. Jean Börlin, to Michel Fokine, 17 June 1918 in *MGZM-Res (Jean Börlin Manuscripts), Dance Collection, New York Public Library.

37. The program for this "Concert de danses" is in the collection of the Dansmuseet, Stockholm. An unsigned review of the concert published in the *London Times* lists most of the dances as well as identifying their composers ("A New Swedish Dancer. M. Börlin's Strange Creations," *London Times,* 30 March 1920, 12).

38. Inghelbrecht, *Mouvement contraire: Souvenirs d'un musicien* (Paris: Editions Domat, 1947), 124.

39. Another echo of the Ballets Russes in the program's musical offerings was Alexander Borodin's "Esquisse sur les steppes de l'Asie centrale," which audiences would have associated with the extremely popular *Polovtsian Dances,* choreographed by Fokine in 1909.

40. Häger, *Ballets Suédois,* 12.

41. Ibid.

42. For Wigman, see Susan A. Manning, *Ecstasy and the Demon: Feminism and Nationalism in the Dances of Mary Wigman* (Berkeley: University of California Press, 1993), 62–67.

43. Berthe Trümpy, quoted ibid., 65.

44. Quoted in RoseLee Goldberg, *Performance: Live Art 1909 to the Present* (New York: Abrams, 1979), 42.

45. Quoted ibid, 48.

46. Quoted in Häger, *Ballets Suédois*, 13–14.

47. Pitts Sanborn, "The Swedish Ballet," *Shadowland*, December 1921, 66; Florence Gilliam, "The Swedish Ballet," *The Freeman*, 22 August 1923, 567; Henri Béraud, "Théâtre," *Mercure de France*, 1 July 1921, 192.

48. The term "action-modes" was coined by Elizabeth Selden in *Elements of the Free Dance* (1930). For its relation to Wigman's work, see Manning, 43–4.

49. Quoted in Häger, *Ballets Suédois*, 106.

50. Ibid., 96.

51. J. Lieubal, "Au Théâtre des Champs-Elysées. Saison de Ballets Suédois," *Comoedia illustré*, 20 November 1920, 56.

52. Cocteau is quoted in de Maré, *Les Ballets Suédois*, 60; Wilson, in Frank W.D. Ries, *The Dance Theatre of Jean Cocteau* (Ann Arbor: UMI Research Press, 1986), 83.

53. André Levinson, *La Danse d'aujourd'hui* (Paris: Duchartre et Van Buggenhoudt, 1929), 400–1.

54. Reynaldo Hahn, "Théâtre des Champs-Elysées. Deuxième spectacle des 'Ballets suédois,'" *Excelsior*, 10 November 1920, File 13 (Ballets Suédois), Valentine Hugo Collection, Theatre Museum (London).

55. W. J. Turner, "The Swedish Ballet," *The New Statesman*, 25 December 1920, 367; "The Sitter Out," *The Dancing Times*, January 1921, 310.

56. Florence Gilliam, "Ballet Suedois — A Unique Stage Spectacle," *Theatre Magazine*, November 1923, 64.

57. Gilliam, "The Swedish Ballet," *The Freeman*, 566. In *Skating Rink*, Levinson wrote in *La Danse d'aujourd'hui*, Borlin, "posed in 'attitude,' obstinately executed little turns en dedans, while around him the action languished, broke up, and melted away" (394); in *Marchand d'oiseaux*, he "made a very graceful entrance with his two cages, then, having disposed of the cages, he posed in attitude and did some little turns en dedans" (396).

58. Gilliam, "The Swedish Ballet," 566.

59. Gilliam, "Parade," 5.

60. Häger, *Ballets Suédois*, 232.

61. De Maré, *Les Ballets Suédois*, 33.

62. Häger, *Ballets Suédois*, 44.

FERNAND LÉGER and the BALLETS SUÉDOIS

THE CONVERGENCE OF AVANT-GARDE AMBITIONS AND COLLABORATIVE IDEALS

Judi Freeman

When Rolf de Maré invited Fernand Léger in 1921 to participate in the creation of the ballet *Skating Rink*, it was by no means a sudden decision. De Maré had been a prewar admirer of Léger's work. He had purchased a major painting—Léger's 1914 *L'Escalier*—in 1915 and continued to acquire works by the artist thereafter. De Maré's principal guide in Parisian artistic circles was a fellow Swede, artist Nils Dardel, who arranged de Maré's art purchases as early as 1914 and subsequently served as one of the designers for de Maré's Ballets Suédois.[1]

The invitation to Léger was a bold step by de Maré into the postcubist aesthetic of the 1920s; his subsequent approach to Francis Picabia, which resulted in *Relâche* (Cancelled), would be an equivalent move into the even more cutting edge world of dada. It was equal in importance, certainly, to Serge Diaghilev enlisting Pablo Picasso in the creation of *Parade*, and was as significant for the visual arts as the score produced by members of Les Six for de Maré's *Les Mariés de la Tour Eiffel* (The Newlyweds on the Eiffel Tower) was for the musical world. "Jean Börlin's three great creations are *Skating Rink*, *Les Mariés de la Tour Eiffel* and the Negro ballet, *La Création du monde*," wrote the poet Blaise Cendrars, with some bias, given his authorship of the scenario for *Création*.[2]

Rolf de Maré acquired a seven-year lease on the Théâtre des Champs-Elysées in 1920 from the financially ailing Gabriel Astruc. "[The theater] in Paris was essential to us," de Maré recalled, "because Paris would become our center, a grand theater in which to be able to develop freely and to present a season of performances; in other words, a large studio was indispensable to our preparations."[3] The acquisition effectively placed him in charge of one of the most prominent theaters in Paris. The Ballets Russes appeared there, as did numerous other performing groups.

While de Maré's place in history has been secured by his founding of the Ballets Suédois, his ambitions were great; he was responsible for booking some of the most diverse and exciting performers in Paris. He was the first to present Anna Pavlova in a Paris music hall and the first to present Josephine Baker on a Paris stage. He enabled Cécile Sorel to perform in the theater and sponsored poetry readings by Maurice Rostand, Paul Fort, and Colette. He tried, though unsuccessfully, to persuade Charlie Chaplin to perform at the Théâtre des Champs-Elysées in October and November of 1924.[4] He also underwrote the publication of the magazines *La Danse*, *Le Théâtre*, and *Le Comoedia illustré*, several of which served intermittently as elaborate programs for performances at the theater.

Fig. 28
FERNAND LÉGER
Costume design for a human figure in *La Création du monde*, 1923, cat. no. 91.

De Maré was a hands-on owner/director, which inevitably led to friction. His nominal theater manager, Jacques Hébertot, played a much larger role simply because de Maré was often traveling. For example, in March 1921 Hébertot met with Diaghilev to discuss the fee the theater would pay for the Ballets Russes performances, since they also performed at the Théâtre des Champs-Elysées. He expressed concern to de Maré, who was in Madrid, that if he negotiated too strongly with Diaghilev they might lose the Ballets Russes to the Paris Opéra. He explained that it would not be good for the Ballets Suédois and the Ballets Russes to perform at the same time.[5] Nor did he feel, following a discussion with Diaghilev in April, that the latter's request for six gala performances was wise, financially or artistically.[6] Hébertot solicited de Maré's advice, but it is clear from his numerous queries and demands that he ultimately made many decisions as well. No doubt this increased the tension between the two, which led to Hébertot's dismissal in 1924.[7]

Erik Satie and André Derain visited Hébertot in July 1921 armed with a proposal. "The pair came together to propose for me a ballet for the Suédois: a new type of ballet and one that is amusing enough, to be sure," wrote Hébertot to de Maré. "I told them that I would relay their idea to you and here it is:

This would be a parody of the Cinema. The backdrop would be created by a projection on a screen that would fill up the entire background; the sides would be of dark fabric. The characters would have the appearance of emerging from the screen, all in black and white, to create a truly cinematic scene. There would be seven or eight different scenes, easy to obtain by simply changing the projection; and we would mock the cinema through exaggerated gestures, speed, and music which would never be in sync with that which was represented.[8]

Derain and Satie's idea was daring and unprecedented in its ambitions. The ideas of combining film and performance on stage and playing with the emergence of one form from another were radical ones.

Derain had just completed working with Diaghilev in 1919 on *La Boutique fantasque*. His highly decorative and colorful costume designs were appropriate to the subject and the production, particularly Derain's contribution to it, was well received in the press. Although the ballet was relatively successful for the Ballets Russes, Derain did not feel comfortable approaching Diaghilev about his new project.[9] With Satie he approached the Ballets Suédois, which by July 1921 was receiving much good press, sometimes to the detriment of the Ballets Russes. "The Théâtre des Champs-Elysées has presented the third program of the Ballets Suédois," J. d'Argency reported in *Revue Mondiale* of December 1920. "This spectacle is entirely admirable, and Monsieur Börlin has conquered Paris as Nijinsky had done before the war."[10]

The Ballets Suédois also had achieved a reputation for a willingness to be more daring and experimental than its rival, thanks to *Les Mariés de la Tour Eiffel*, which was essentially a retort to *Parade*.[11] Its author, Jean Cocteau, discussed the planned production in the June 1921 issue of *La Danse*. He argued that the new project continued the tradition of his work on *Parade* and *Le Boeuf sur le toit* (The Nothing-Happens Bar, a musical production he mounted in 1920 at the Comédie des Champs-Elysées, with music by Darius Milhaud and under the aegis of Count Etienne de Beaumont.[12] He defined the production by what it was not: "Ballet? No. Play? No. Revue? No. Tragedy? No. Rather a sort of secret marriage between ancient tragedy and the year-end revue, the Greek chorus and the music-hall number."[13] By enlisting Cocteau and all but one member of Les Six, by parodying French culture (as opposed to *Parade*'s spoof on American society), the Ballets Suédois sent a clear message of their intention to move beyond conventional dance.

Though the project was realized neither in the form Hébertot described nor for the Ballets Suédois, the proposal indicates that the company was considered receptive to this type of production.[14] At the time, the Ballets Russes was thoroughly committed to certain Russian artists (Léon Bakst, Alexandre Benois, Natalia Gontcharova, Mikhail Larionov) and to French artists—generally those, such as Henri Matisse, Picasso, and Robert and Sonia Delaunay, who had achieved some degree of success and attention during the prewar period. Shortly after Derain and Satie's visit Hébertot noted that the Ballets Suédois was at the center of conversation among a slightly younger and more international generation of avant-garde painters. At the dinner following Nils Dardel's July 1921 wedding, Hébertot reported, "I was alongside Léger and other painters who often spoke about the Ballets Suédois in entirely excellent and warm terms. Léger spoke to me at length about *Nuit de Saint Jean* (Saint John's Night, or Midsummer Night's Revel), telling me that with *Les Vierges folles*, (The Foolish Virgins) this was that what he believed to be the best of the Suédois."[15]

Léger avidly followed the activities of the theater world. Even while actively serving in Argonne in 1916 Léger discussed with his future wife, Jeanne Lohy, the

Fig. 1
FERNAND LÉGER
Costume design for a Sailor in blue and red in *Skating Rink*, 1921, cat. no. 74.

possibility that he might design for the stage. When she suggested that he propose a production to Diaghilev he initially dismissed the idea as the "fantasies of a very rich woman."[16] Nevertheless he continued to be intrigued by the notion; in a letter several weeks later he urged Jeanne to visit Diaghilev in case a letter from Gontcharova, presumably concerning Léger's work, had not reached him: "He may need to have information about me. It is necessary that you go there. A little bit of courage. . . Diaghilev is a serious matter."[17]

After the war, Léger stopped in London while on a trip to Oslo and saw the Ballets Russes perform there. To Ragnar Hoppe, the curator of the Royal Museum (soon to become the Nationalmuseum) in Stockholm, he wrote: "We have found the Ballets Russes a complete success here. I have had a box available to me and we have judged the Derain ballet pleasant—with [Léonide] Massine in his box, I saw Matisse, Jacques Blanche—all of Paris!"[18] Léger's overt and more subtle approaches to Diaghilev were ultimately unrequited, but they reveal his thinking during and immediately after the war.

Léger undoubtedly was aware of plans for the creation of the Ballets Suédois at their inception. During the war he remained in close contact with Nils Dardel, whom he had first met in Paris in 1910. While at the front he was grateful for and very much dependent on Dardel's purchases of his work.[19] Some time in the course of his growing acquaintance with Dardel, Léger met de Maré. He refers to him as the "Comte Suédois" in a November 1915 letter to Jeanne and mentions writing to him shortly thereafter.[20] In March 1916 Léger mentions de Maré and Dardel together and marvels at their relationship: "It's very funny, this combination of de Maré and Dardel. I do not understand it very well within this entire business. It is above all the payments by account that amaze me. I know that with you Dardel

Fig. 2
FERNAND LÉGER
Costume design for a woman in checked skirt in *Skating Rink*, 1921, cat. no. 76.

Fig. 3
FERNAND LÉGER
Costume design for a woman in white, blue, and brown in *Skating Rink*, 1921, cat. no. 68.

behaves like a pal. But all the same it's funny. I ask myself if he will give you the 100 francs and at one time; I don't believe so. I believe that Rolf gives him money and [Nils] keeps it and pays it out in small amounts."[21] Subsequently he seems unusually aware of de Maré's whereabouts: "You know I believe that Mr Rolf de Maré is on a boat. If his painting is not paid for one will dispose of it somehow . . . these millionaires behave as if they are impressing [us] with a thousand note!"[22]

De Maré's acquisition of Léger's *L'Escalier* in early 1915,[23] followed by Dardel's purchase of his *Le Soldat à la pipe* (1916),[24] indicates that just as Léger maintained an ongoing awareness of de Maré's doings, de Maré reciprocated the interest. Dardel purchased for de Maré a small, highly personal picture by Léger, *La Partie des cartes* (1915), a work that would only appeal to a collector already committed to an artist.[25] In late 1919 or early 1920, Dardel, once again acting on de Maré's behalf, purchased Léger's *Le Pont de bateau* (1919) from Léonce Rosenberg, Léger's dealer.[26]

De Maré and Dardel were likely to have known directly from the artist of Léger's evolving ideas on spectacle and performance, although these were not published in article form before 1922. An appropriate project for the painter emerged thanks to the writer and critic Ricciotto Canudo.

Canudo was not a newcomer to the theatrical world. He had written on theater and ballet for a number of years, notably in his 1907 book *Le Livre de l'évolution*. A 1911 essay advocated that dance be "an art of synthesis and not solely choreographic entertainment" and expressed his desire for "the perfect harmony of all elements of performance."[27] Canudo most assuredly paid considerable attention to the Ballets Suédois, particularly given the like-minded articulation of the company's mission beginning with its earliest programs. In November 1920 Canudo published an article in *La Revue de l'époque* on the music hall at the Théâtre des Champs Elysees that Hébertot and probably de Maré read, thanks in no small part to their thorough clipping service.[28] Hébertot contacted Canudo, who immediately replied that he had intended to write about the Ballets Suédois in the same article but did not have an opportunity to do so. He was planning to write on the company in the next issue of the review: "You may count on my loyalty and that of my friends," he assured Hébertot.[29]

On the occasion of Canudo's death at the age of 44 in November 1923 de Maré offered the following comments:

patiné" and "Charlot patinage."

In *The Rink* Chaplin accompanies a sweetheart to the skating rink and despite several amusing pratfalls and mishaps displays his talents on the ice. He collides with a bully, a rival for his girl's affections. A quickfire Keystone Cops–inspired melée ensues. Following some fast dodges and swift getaways, Charlot emerges triumphant, shuffling off to live happily ever after. Canudo's *Skating Rink* adopted the basic plot of Chaplin's film, but elaborated on its sketchier details. The central character becomes both meditative poet and naive fool, much like Chaplin's tramp character. He moves amid a large crowd of skating couples, perpetually circling the rink. A lone woman emerges from the crowd. Attracted by the poet's red scarf, she joins him. They dance, then are interrupted by a madman-bully, who is "inflamed with jealous anger," in Canudo's scenario. The men engage in the inevitable battle with its sad conclusion: the poet loses the girl to the bully and is absorbed by the swirling crowd.

Léger later recalled how the poet Guillaume Apollinaire took him to see a Chaplin film for the first time while both were on leave from the front lines during the First World War.[39] He was especially receptive to Canudo's Charlot references and freely embraced them in his conception for the design. Indeed the people in Léger's studies for *Skating Rink* closely resemble the populace of his concurrent paintings of farmers and city dwellers: they are interchangeable, generally uniform, sometimes faceless. The Charlot figure also served as the subject of Léger's illustrations for Ivan Goll's "Die Chaplinade" (1920), as the focus of his three wooden reliefs *Charlot cubiste* (1923), and in the image that opened and closed his 1924 film *Ballet mécanique*.

Contemplating the social function of the skating rink, Léger visited comparable dance halls and bals musettes as well as the rink at the Vélodrome d'Hiver, often accompanied by de Maré and Börlin (Fig. 15).[40] As a place of leisure, an essential feature of a world dominated by work and the machine, the rink for him was a place where all types of people convened to share a common pastime. His backdrop for the ballet (Fig. 16) unified this diverse crowd in a melange of geometric forms and blocks of bold color, which closely resembled his contemporary paintings called *Eléments mécaniques*. The upper half contained a wide arc of brightly colored geometric shapes, with the word RING subtly formed in stencil lettering, recalling similar usages in paintings such as *La Ville* (1919). The lower half remained empty, to be animated by dancing figures—"moving scenery," as he called them.[41] In his final design for the curtain (Fig. 17) these dancing figures are integrated with the geometric shapes, suggesting Léger's vision of the interplay of kinetic and static elements.

Fig. 15
Fernand Léger and Rolf de Maré at the Bal Musette music hall, Paris, 1921, cat. no. 220.

Léger's designs were crucial to Börlin's choreography; two previously unidentified sketches of choreographic notation indicate that he conceived his movement based on already completed costumes (Fig. 18). Under considerable pressure to choreograph the ballet while on tour with the company, Börlin seems to have rapidly outlined possible movements within the framework of Léger's relatively restrictive costume designs. The steps he conceived were jerky in nature, rigidly synchronized, and largely planar.

Despite Léger's attempt to make a powerful statement with his sets and costumes, the critics who attended the opening on 22 January 1922 paid little attention to his work. Reviewers for *Le Menestrel*, *Comoedia*, *L'Université de Paris*, *Le Monde illustré*, *L'Opinion*, *Le Petit bleu*, and *L'Intransigéant*, all of whom covered the ballet at length, barely mentioned the sets and costumes. This

Fig. 16
FERNAND LÉGER
Backdrop design for *Skating Rink*, 1921, cat. no. 60.

can perhaps be attributed to the preponderance of music critics who reviewed ballet for French newspapers and journals; for instance, when critic and conductor Emile Vuillermoz reviewed *Skating Rink*, he interpreted Léger's role as that of dressing Honegger's work: "A painter was invited to play a new game on this same theme. Monsieur Fernand Léger, and I will not permit myself to judge his talent, will not contradict me if I indicate that nothing [he has created], in his conscientious and organized Cubist technique, is chosen to 'dress' a work by Honegger."[42]

Léger had sought a truly collaborative enterprise but instead was enlisted late in the venture and asked to quickly invent the look of the ballet. The fact that Honegger was in Zurich and Börlin and de Maré were on tour in the French provinces was for Léger a great impediment to producing a successful ballet. Léger could not give a dancer a tight sleeve or high collar without knowing how that dancer's body would move; he could not decide on a flat or circular backdrop without determining how the choreography would convey the illusion of the rink or of skating. He concluded that the collaborators had to create the ballet together, simultaneously. He needed to realize all aspects of the ballet not in isolation, but in a sort of ideal communion with other creators.[43] Frustrated but undaunted, he sought a more fully collaborative venture.

La Création du monde fulfilled Léger's hopes in this regard. Its evolution differed in several significant respects from that of *Skating Rink*. Léger and the author, Cendrars, proposed the project to de Maré and Börlin at the outset.[44] Cendrars's 1921 book, *Anthologie nègre*, a compilation of tales from various African tribes, served as the textual basis. One of the creation myths told of three gods—Nzamé, Mébère, and Nkwa—who created the sky, earth, animals, plants, the order of living things, and, finally, the first man and woman. It was this final portion of the legend that Cendrars adapted for the ballet.[45] Initially it was to be a *séance nègre*, a collection of ten tribal dances, but by the summer of 1922, when Cendrars and Léger produced a detailed outline, it had become a more developed *ballet nègre*, with a clear narrative and precise staging instructions.[46]

Léger's ambitions for *La Création du monde* matched de Maré's desire for something utterly new and revelatory on the stage. If *Les Mariés de la Tour Eiffel* had been

Fig. 17
FERNAND LÉGER
Curtain design for *Skating Rink*, 1921, cat. no. 59.

Fig. 18
JEAN BÖRLIN
Choreographic notation for *Skating Rink*, 1921, cat. no. 156.

Fig. 19
FERNAND LÉGER
Figure study for *La Création du monde*, 1923, cat. no. 96.

Fig. 20
FERNAND LÉGER
Backdrop design for *La Création du monde*, 1923, cat. no. 78.

the Ballets Suédois's response to *Parade*, *La Création du monde* resonated with the memory of the Ballets Russes's 1913 *Le Sacre du printemps*. Léger now became more assertive. "You know that we think of making an important and extremely calculated work. It should be the only possible *ballet nègre* in the entire world and to be that which endures as definitive of the genre," he extolled. He emphasized the need for close collaboration: "It requires a multifarious, very meticulous spirit among Cendrars, Börlin, and me."[47] Instead of waiting for de Maré and Börlin to select a composer, Léger, along with Cendrars, first recommended Satie. When they learned Satie was unavailable, they selected Darius Milhaud, who had composed the score for *L'Homme et son désir* (Man and His Desire) and had worked with the company on *Les Mariés de la Tour Eiffel* as a member of Les Six.[48]

Léger knew Cendrars extremely well. They had traveled in the same artistic circles before the war and had kept in touch with one another during it, when Cendrars was severely wounded and had his right arm amputated. Léger illustrated the first edition of Cendrars's *J'ai tué* (1918), designed and illustrated his *La fin du monde filmée par l'Ange N[otre]-D[ame]* (1919), and worked with him on Abel Gance's film, *La Roue*. The two insisted on nearly eighteen months of preparation before the ballet's premiere on 22 October 1923. "This is an important work to which Cendrars and I will devote all our evenings," Léger wrote de Maré.[49]

As part of his research for the masks for *La Création du monde*, Léger hoped to study at the British Museum, but he never made the trip. Instead he filled a notebook with pencil sketches of African sculptures in Parisian collections. In addition to the examples at the Musée d'Ethnographie Léger saw Alphonse Kann's and Paul Guillaume's rich collections of primitive art. He made numerous studies of dolls, masks, and full figures based on these direct sources and on illustrations in books on African sculpture by Carl Einstein and Marius de Zayas.[50]

Concurrently Léger and Cendrars reworked the

Fig. 21
FERNAND LÉGER
Set design for *La Création du monde*, 1923, cat. no. 79.

Fig. 22
La Création du monde, Paris, 1923, cat. no. 225.

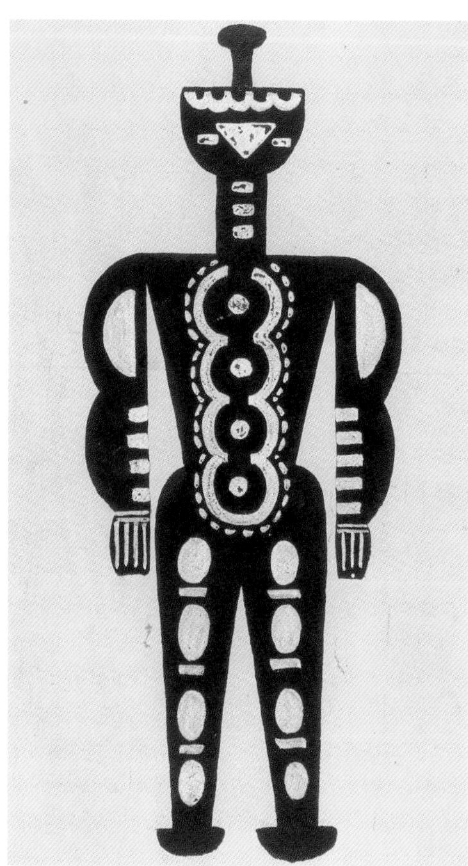

Fig. 23
FERNAND LÉGER
Costume design for the First Man in *La Création du monde*, 1923, cat. no. 85.

Fig. 24
FERNAND LÉGER
Costume design for an archaic being in *La Création du monde*, 1923, cat. no. 90.

Fig. 25
FERNAND LÉGER
Costume design for a Monkey in *La Création du monde*, 1923, cat. no. 87.

original scenario to make it more stageworthy. They divided the narrative into twelve sections, making notes for the stagehands and rough choreographic arrangements. They specified lighting colors and suggested musical types—valses, pavannes—for each segment.[51]

As was his practice, Léger immersed himself in the search for material. He, Cendrars, and Milhaud visited dance halls and clubs. The experience profoundly influenced Milhaud. He used a seventeen-piece orchestra, identical to one he had seen in Harlem, to perform the jazz-infused scores. Jazz, wrote Milhaud, "had its roots in the darkest corners of the negro soul, the vestigal traces of Africa no doubt. Its effect on me was so overwhelming that I could not tear myself away."[52]

Léger's boundless imagination quickly became evident. He proposed, for example, that inflated flowers, trees, and various animals be sent up into the air at the moment of the world's creation. In the end this concept was abandoned because the necessary machinery was complex and costly and the sound of the required gas would have been disruptive. Léger, with Cendrars, also envisioned a sun and a moon, but once realized, these were never sufficiently visible to be seen from the audience.[53] Ultimately he pursued more conventional designs, remaining faithful to the general outlines of African sculpture but making them into mechanocubist figures (Fig. 19). These became particularly hieratic in studies for the ballet's backdrops and sets. Léger initially began with strongly cubist forms that in the end were used as moving characters on the stage. These were especially mechanomorphic when seen set against the open, unpopulated landscape of a virgin world (Figs. 20-22). The gods depicted on the curtain became magnified heads, often with their bodies eliminated and all sense of setting discarded.

Léger limited his colors largely to ochers, browns, blacks, and whites—earth colors suggesting the primordial world. The figures were extremely abstract; the first man (Fig. 23) and woman were at once primitive and futurist in conception. Animals (Figs. 24–25) took on a surreal appearance, fantastic and ferocious. Birds (Figs. 26–27) were over seven feet in height and featured a dizzying array of colors. From this exotic world emerged the human figures, in appearance a cross between primitive sculpture and calligraphic renderings of jazz-age figures (Fig. 28). Léger gradually matched the characters to Milhaud's music. He later described "these large ocher, black, and white surfaces roughly breaking up the remarkable equilibrium which otherwise occurs in Milhaud's score," and envisioned how the curtain

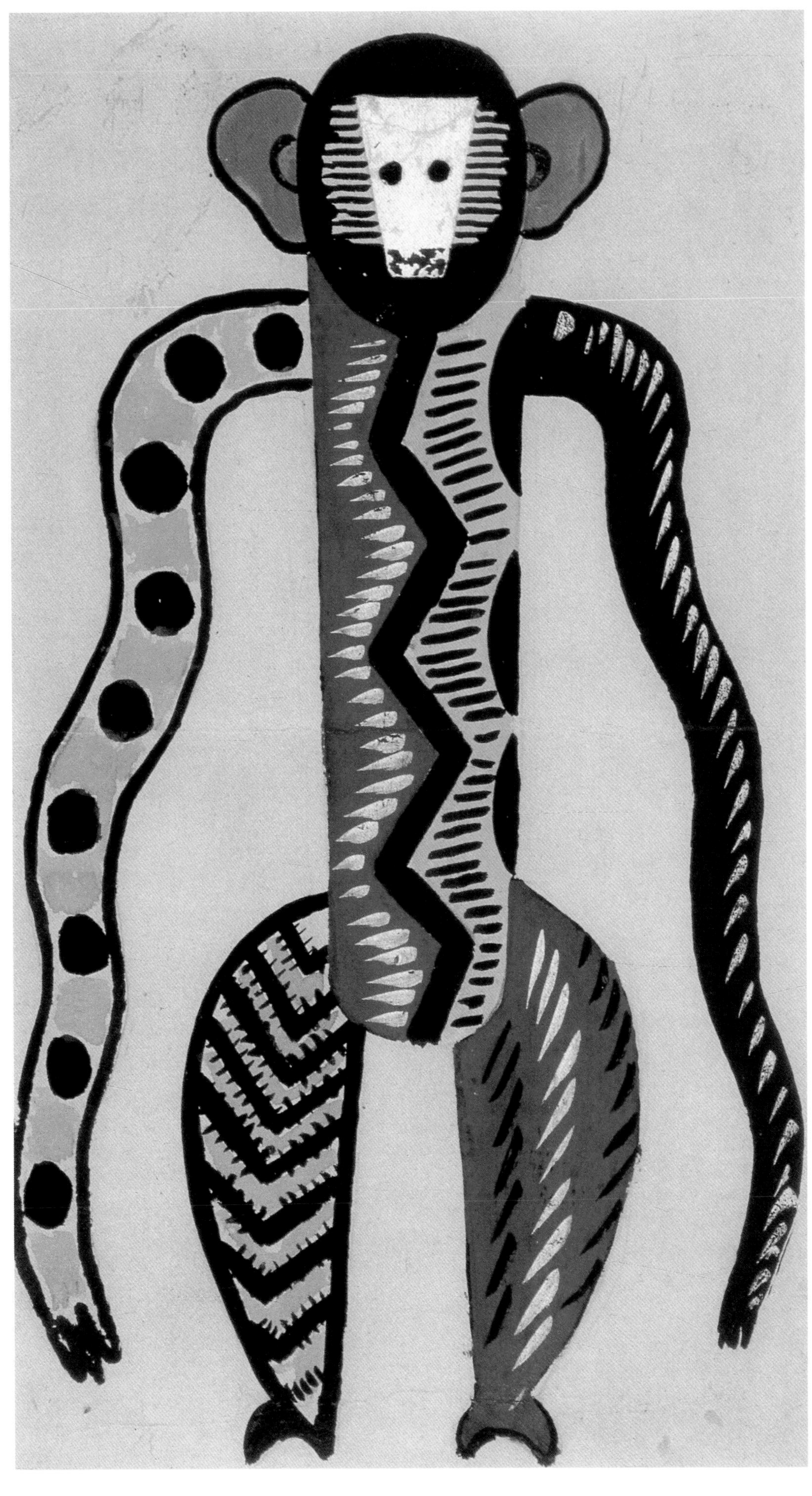

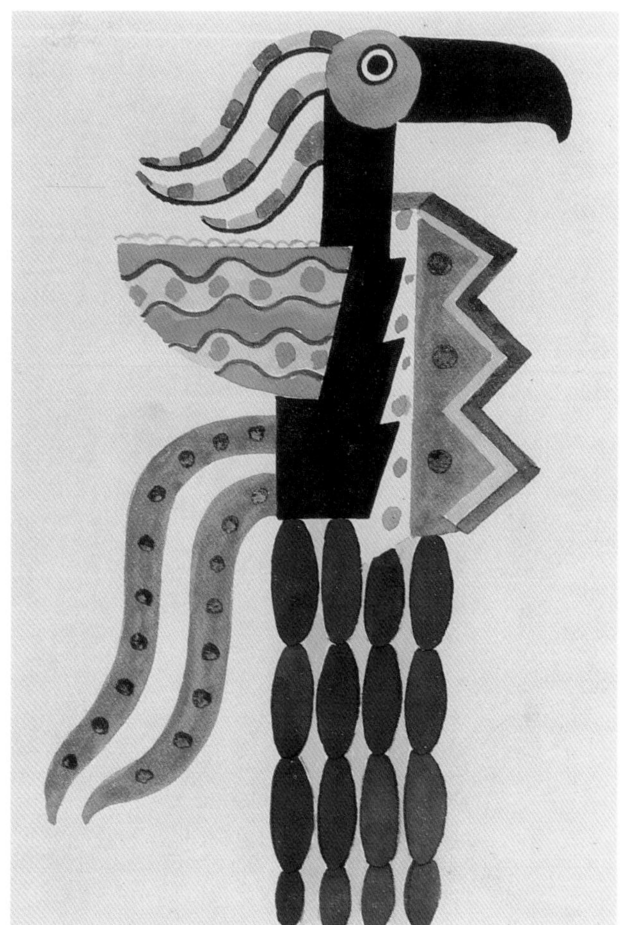

Fig. 26–27
FERNAND LÉGER
Costume designs for Birds in *La Création du monde*, 1923, cat. nos. 99 and 101.

would rise with the "fluttering of trumpets, the repeated melody of the saxophone."[54]

During the three months prior to the premiere Léger supervised the construction of the sets and curtain as well as the execution of the costumes and props. The costumes were bulky and cumbersome and needed to be precisely fitted to accomodate the movements, however limited, of the performers.

Börlin during this period worked on the choreography. In his solo performance of *Sculpture nègre* at the Comédie des Champs-Elysées in March 1920 he wore a mask and constricting clothing; consequently he already had experience in employing the stiff poses of African statuary. Any more detailed movement he created would be largely obscured by Léger's massive costume constructions.

Though no doubt the ballet posed many problems for the company, it captured the attention of the public. Generally the reviews were positive and Léger's designs, thanks to their sheer dominance of the stage, were usually discussed. Léger was elated:

The modern stage can go this far; we have the means to do it. The public will follow, it has followed; proof is there. I wish to pay homage here to Rolf de Maré, director of the Ballets Suédois, who was the first person in France to have the courage to agree to a performance in which everything is done with machinery and the play of light, where no human silhouette is on the stage; and to Jean Börlin and his troupe, who are condemned to the role of moving scenery. . . . In agreeing to perform the ballet nègre La Création du monde *he dared to impose on the public for the first time a truly modern theater, at least in terms of technical means. His effort was rewarded with success. The public followed him openly, directly.*[55]

Léger remained euphoric about the potential of ballet and the stage in general. Throughout early 1924 he visited Hébertot frequently, offering suggestions about the presentation of *La Création du monde* during the Ballets Suédois's tour to the United States later that year.

He accompanied Gerald Murphy, who would design *Within the Quota* for the company, to meet with Börlin and Hébertot. Cendrars, meanwhile, began a collaboration with Satie on a ballet which ultimately would be realized (minus Cendrars) by Satie in the form of *Relâche*, in partnership with artist Francis Picabia and fledgling filmmaker René Clair.[56] But Léger continued to conjure up fantastical stage effects:

The impact of parallel forces (20 performers moving together).

Contrasting forces can operate to the maximum.

Ten yellow acrobats cross the stage (fast rhythm) doing cartwheels, they return (same rhythm), the stage is dark; they are phosphorescent; at the same time (slower rhythm) the film projector energizes the top of the set, raises the back curtain; the apparition of the beautiful object, moving or unmoving, that holds the stage. Time X. The staircase, the cartwheel, the display of unexpected invention that glitters and disappears.

To conceive of objects as the pivot of interest, objects so beautiful that they have an enormous spectacle value, unknown and always sacrificed to the eternal star.[57]

The demise of the Ballets Suédois in March 1925 did not curb Léger's appetite for the stage. Though Léger and the French avant-garde lamented the disappearance of the company, he remained ever idealistic, writing essays on theatrical spectacle as well as many scenario drafts that were never realized. He continued to correspond with de Maré throughout the 1930s. The company's dissolution coincided with the diminution of other companies, such as the Ballets Russes and Etienne de Beaumont's Soirées de Paris. After 1925 there were fewer opportunities for avant-garde Parisian artists to work on the stage and fewer experimental vehicles in other media. The distinguished dealer Léonce Rosenberg reminded de Maré that the Ballets Suédois had "given exceptional service to modern art and to each of us some genuine, considerable happiness . . . for you personally and for your work, the highest distinction for our affection and our gratitude."[58]

All translations are by the author unless otherwise noted.

1. Nils Dardel purchased for de Maré three works by Georges Braque, two by Pablo Picasso, and one each by Paul Gauguin, Odilon Redon, and Georges Seurat from Alfred Flechtheim in Düsseldorf in August 1914. In July of that same year, he purchased a Picasso and a Juan Gris from Wilhelm von Uhde in Paris. His purchases actively resumed in May 1920 when he bought the Léger as well as a Braque (*Nature morte*, 1919) from Léonce Rosenberg's Galerie de l'Effort Moderne. Two months earlier, Walther Halvorsen, a Norwegian art critic and erstwhile dealer, had purchased works by Honoré Daumier, Gustave Courbet, and Georges Seurat for de Maré.

2. "Les trois grandes créations de Jean Börlin sont *Skating-Rink*, *Les Mariés de la Tour Eiffel* et le ballet nègre, *La Création du monde*," in Blaise Cendrars, manuscript of a biography of Jean Börlin, n.d.; Dansmuseet, Stockholm.

3. "Il nous fallait une scène à Paris, car Paris devait devenir notre centre, un grand théâtre pour pouvoir évoluer librement et y donner une saison; en outre, un grand studio nous était indispensable pour les recherches." Rolf de Maré, cited in Pierre Tugal, "Les Ballets Suédois expression d'une époque." *Les Ballets Suédois dans l'art contemporain* (Paris: Editions du Trianon, 1931), 27.

4. Hébertot to Rolf de Maré, 12 and 15 February 1924; Dansmuseet, Stockholm.

5. Hébertot to Rolf de Maré, Paris, 10 March 1921; Dansmuseet, Stockholm.

6. Hébertot to Rolf de Maré, Paris, 4 April 1921; Dansmuseet, Stockholm.

7. Hébertot was held responsible for missing ticket receipts and other fiscal irregularities and was dismissed.

8. "Ils venaient tous les deux me proposer un ballet pour les Suédois: un ballet d'un nouveau genre et qui est assez amusant, ma foi. Je leur ai dit que je te soumettrais l'idée et la voici: Ce serait une parodie du Cinéma. Le décor du fond serait fait par une projection donnée sur un écran, qui remplirait tout le fond de la scène, les côtés étant d'étoffe sombre. Les personnages auraient donc l'air de sortir de l'écran tous en blanc et noir pour faire une vraie scène de cinéma. Il y aurait sept ou huit scènes différentes, faciles à obtenir par le simple changement d'une projection et on se moquerait du cinéma dans l'exagération des gestes, la vitesse et par la musique qui ne serait pour ainsi dire jamais en rapport avec ce qu'on représenterait." Hébertot to Rolf de Maré, 13 July 1921, Dansmuseet, Stockholm.

9. This may well be because Derain was Diaghilev's third choice as the ballet's designer. Léon Bakst had been first, but the two had a falling out. Mikhail Larionov was also approached and made some preliminary designs, but these were ultimately not accepted. It may also be because there were numerous complaints about Derain's obvious inexperience in the theater. Serge Grigoriev complained about the unsuitability of the designs; see Grigoriev, *The Diaghilev Ballet, 1909–1929*, ed. and trans. Vera Bowen (London: Harmondsworth, 1960), 154.

10. "Le Théâtre des Champs-Elysées a donné son troisième spectacle des Ballets Suédois. Ce spectacle est absolument admirable, et M. Borlin a conquis Paris comme Nijinsky avait conquis avant la guerre." J. d'Argency in *Revue Mondiale*, 1 December 1920.

11. It has been suggested that Derain was influenced by the

designs for Ballets Suédois production of *Les Mariés de la Tour Eiffel* in creating the masks for his ballet *Les Songes* (1933). See Philippe Chabert, "André Derain, homme de théâtre," in *André Derain: Le peintre du 'trouble moderne'*, exh. cat. (Paris: Musée d'art moderne de la ville de Paris, 1994), 358.

12. On other occasions Cocteau contended that *Les Mariés de la Tour Eiffel* was distinctly separate from his previous works: "Until *Les Mariés de la Tour Eiffel*, the first work in which I owe nothing to anyone, which resembles no other work, where I found my formula, I forced the lock and twisted my key in all directions." Cocteau, *La Difficulté d'être* (Monaco: Editions du Rocher, 1953), 21. In Neal Oxenhandler, *Scandal & Parade: The Theatre of Jean Cocteau* (New Brunswick, New Jersey: Rutgers University Press, 1957), 49.

13. "Ballet? non. Pièce? non. Revue? non. Tragédie? non. Plutôt une sorte de mariage secret entre la tragédie antique et la revue de fin d'année, le choeur et le numéro de music-hall." Cocteau, "A Vol d'oiseau sur *Les Mariés de la Tour Eiffel*," *La Danse*, June 1921, n.p.

14. Aspects of the proposal, however, found their way into Derain's *Jack in the Box*, staged in 1926 by Etienne de Beaumont's Soirées de Paris in May 1926 at the Théâtre des Champs-Elysées. Music was by Satie and choreography was by the young George Balanchine. Several weeks later it was performed by the Ballets Russes at the Théâtre Sarah Bernhardt. See decor and related drawings in the Serge Lifar collection at the Wadsworth Atheneum, Hartford.

15. "J'étais à côté de Léger et d'autres peintres qui ont beaucoup parlé des Ballets-Suédois, en des termes tout-à-fait excellents et chauds. Léger m'a longuement parlé de *Nuit de Saint-Jean*, en me disant qu'avec *Vierges folles*, c'était ce qu'il considérait comme meilleur dans les Suédois." Hébertot to Rolf de Maré, 26 July 1921; Dansmuseet, Stockholm.

16. "[F]antaisies de femme très riche." Léger, letter to Jeanne Lohy, Champagne, 6 January 1917; Fernand Léger archives. It should be noted that Jeanne Lohy was not wealthy.

17. "[I]l peut avoir besoin de renseignement sur moi. Il faut que tu sois là. Un petit peu de courage. . . . Diaghilev c'est la chose sérieuse." Léger to Jeanne Lohy, Champagne, 17 February 1917; Fernand Léger archives. Léger's relationship with both Natalia Gontcharova and her husband Mikhail Larionov is of considerable interest and has to date not been extensively researched. It is clear that Léger (via Jeanne) was in frequent correspondence with both artists, especially Gontcharova, during the war. Léger was especially eager to exhibit with the pair.

18. "Nous avons trouvé ici les Ballets Russes en plein succès. J'ai eu un loge à ma disposition et nous avons apprecié le ballet Derain agréable—chez Massine dans sa loge, vu Matisse Jacques Blanche—Tout Paris!" Léger, postcard (of Windsor Castle) to Ragnar Hoppe, London, 24 November 1919; Ragnar Hoppe collection, Lundsuniversitet, Lund, Sweden.

Léger had a one-person exhibition in Oslo at Tivoli, from 25 October to 10 November, 1919.

19. Léger wrote to Dardel in 1915: "I am very flattered that one of my paintings made here had pleased you and that you have acquired it. These paintings made at the front are certainly rather rare in my oeuvre. I did not consider selling them, but the circumstances have made me somewhat obliged to do so. The others were for the most part with collectors or dealers. Only those made a month before the war in Normandy are still at my disposal. I understand that you would be interested in seeing them. These are the rather abstract researches (contrasts of forms and colors) that I sought to realize in a large painting that has the title *L'Escalier*. The war has seized me and has prevented me from realizing that which I desire. If luck permits me to continue working, I will return to these with force and pleasure. The war has seized me too late to influence me. I will continue the same effort with the same tendencies." ("Je suis très flatté qu'un de mes tableaux fait ici vous ait plu et que vous en ayez fait l'acquisition. Ces tableaux faits sur le front seront certainement assez rares dans mon oeuvre. Je ne tenais pas à les vendre, mais les circonstances m'y ont un peu obligé. Les autres étant pour la plupart chez des collectionneurs ou des marchands. Seuls quelques-uns faits un mois avant la guerre en Normandie sont encore à ma disposition. J'apprends que vous seriez curieux de les voir. Je vais faire mon possible pour les faire parvenir à Paris. Ce sont des recherches assez abstraites (contrastes de formes et de couleurs) que je cherchais à réaliser dans une grande toile qui aurait eu le titre *L'Escalier*. La guerre m'a pris et m'a empêché de réaliser ce que je voulais. Si la chance me permet de continuer mes travaux, je m'y remettrai avec force et plaisir. La guerre m'a pris trop tard pour m'influencer. Je continuerai le même effort avec les mêmes tendances.") Léger to Nils Dardel, Argonne, 14 November 1915; Archives Thora Dardel-Hamilton, Stockholm.

Letters from Léger to Jeanne Lohy indicate that he was eager to receive news of Dardel's purchases and payments. Léger was most concerned about money during this period so that Jeanne could survive financially in Paris. Around 20 February 1916 Léger inquired about Dardel's plans to exhibit several of his pictures in Sweden. "You will be busy with the Swedish exhibition when Dardel will be there and when you will have the funds." ("T'occuperas de l'exposition de Suède quand Dardel sera là et que tu auras l'argent"); Léger, letter to Jeanne Lohy, Argonne, 20 February 1916; Fernand Léger archives. A month earlier, he referred to the same exhibition in a letter to his friend Louis Poughon: "The Swedes would like to organize an exhibition for me in their country." ("Les Suédois veulent m'organiser une exposition chez eux.") Léger to Louis Poughon, Argonne, 22 January 1916; Musée national d'art moderne, Centre Georges Pompidou, Paris. An unpublished note in French that appears to be in Dardel's hand lists works that may be the anticipated contents of such an exhibition or that were sent to Sweden by Dardel for sale:

> two paintings made at the front
> 1 artillery horse
> 2 horses...
> 4 ink drawings made at the front
> 4 other drawings
> 2 large charcoal drawings
> of Fernand Léger

(deux tableaux faits au front
1 les chevaux d'artillerie
2 les chevaux . . .
4 dessins à l'encre faits au front
4 autre dessins
2 grands dessins au fusain
de Fernand Léger)

Archives Thora Dardel-Hamilton, Stockholm.

Letters from Dardel to de Maré indicate that the relationship between Jeanne Lohy and Dardel was not a simple one. In March 1916 Dardel wrote, "Rumor has it here that I am Madame Léger's lover and she does not seem at all upset by the talk, but on the contrary has delightedly announced the arrival of letters and telegrams from me. This has disgusted me a great deal. I do all I can to meet her as little as possible. Bloody hell." Several weeks later, after one of Léger's paintings, probably *Le Soldat à la pipe*, was purchased through Jeanne, Dardel wrote to de Maré again: "I have sent Madame Léger her money. She is in the country, thank God. I was at the station and said goodbye to her. Everybody arrived with flowers. I gave her a little monkey instead. She was delighted with it. The blasted woman calls it Nils." Dardel to de Maré, Paris, 29 March 1916; Dansmuseet, Stockholm. See Erik Näslund, "Fernand Léger and the Ballets Suédois," in *Sommarutställning: Fernand Léger och Svenska Baletten ur Dansmuseets samlingar*, exh. cat. (Stockholm: Bukowskis, 1990), 61. (It is worth noting that Jeanne Lohy did not become Mme Léger until she married the artist on 2 December 1919.)

20. Léger to Jeanne Lohy, Argonne, 3 and 22 November 1915; Fernand Léger archives.

21. "C'est très drôle cette combinaison de Rolf Mare *[sic]* et Dardel. J'en y vois pas très clair dans tout cette affaire là. C'est surtout les paiements par compte qui m'éatent. Je sais qu' avec toi Dardel fait comme un copain. Mais tout de même c'est drôle. Je me demande s'il va te donner le 100F et sur seul coup je me crois pas. Je crois ceci Rolf lui a donné l'argent mais lui il le garde et paie par petits paquets." Léger to Jeanne Lohy, Argonne, 27 March 1916; Fernand Léger archives.

22. "Tu sais je crois que Mr Rolf de Maré c'est au bateau. Si son tableau n'est pas payé on en disposera quelque est que ces millionnaires à la manière qu'impressent par trouver un billet de mille!" Léger to Jeanne Lohy, Argonne, 6 May 1916; Fernand Léger archives.

23. De Maré purchased *L'Escalier* (now in the Moderna Museet, Stockholm) for 1500 francs in 1915; see unpublished *Kassa bok (1914–1950)* of Rolf de Maré, Dansmuseet, Stockholm.

It is worth noting that another version of *L'Escalier*, titled *Exit the Ballets Russes* (according to its original owner) was first purchased by Léonide Massine. It was subsequently acquired by the Museum of Modern Art, New York, in 1958.

24. De Maré purchased this painting (now in the Kunstsammlung Nordrhein-Westfalen, Düsseldorf) from Léger for 2,000 francs in 1920; see *Kassa bok (1914–1950)* of Rolf de Maré, Dansmuseet, Stockholm.

25. De Maré (through Dardel) purchased this painting, under the title *En Front*, for 500 francs from Jeanne Lohy, acting on Léger's behalf, in 1916. See *Kassa bok (1914–1950)* of Rolf de Maré, Dansmuseet, Stockholm.

26. De Maré purchased this painting (now in the Moderna Museet, Stockholm) for 1700 francs; see *Kassa bok (1914–1950)* of Rolf de Maré, Dansmuseet, Stockholm. Rosenberg sent Dardel a copy of the bill for two paintings, which were shipped to de Maré at his Swedish country home in Landskrona. Rosenberg to Nils Dardel, Paris, 26 May 1920; Archives Thora Dardel-Hamilton, Stockholm.

27. "[U]n art de synthèse et non plus comme un divertissement chorégraphique" and "l'harmonie parfaite de tous les éléments du spectacle." Canudo, "Ballets russes et snobs latins," *La Renaissance Contemporaine*, 24 August 1911.

28. Canudo, "La Leçon du Music-Hall," *La Revue de l'epoque* 11, 2ème siècle, November 1920.

29. *Le Livre de l'évolution: L'homme (psychologie musicale des civilisations)* (Paris: E. Sansot & Cie, 1907). "[V]ous pouvez compter sur mon fidélité et celle de mes amis." Canudo to Hébertot, Paris, n.d. [probably late January 1921]; Dansmuseet, Stockholm.

30. "On me demande quelques lignes sur Canudo. C'est un livre qu'il faudrait pour le décrire. Un jour, il vint me voir; je ne le connaissais que de nom. C'était pour me dire. 'Voila, de Maré, j'ai un ballet, qu'on pourrait appeler *Skating-Rink.* C'est la lourde mélancholie des plaisirs de skating, cette sorte d'animalité intime que l'on ressent parmi le balancement glissant, ralenti des couples populaires, de tous les types qui évoluent dans ce milieu; en somme, une synthése de tous les instincts.' Canudo parla longuement. Il ne parlait pas, il chantait, il mimait; ses mains s'agitaient fébriles, et je n'écoutais pas ce qu'il disait du ballet, je regardais cet homme." De Maré, unpublished typewritten manuscript, n.d. [probably end 1923 or early 1924]; Dansmuseet, Stockholm. See also Giovanni Lista, "Canudo e il teatro," *Ricciotto Canudo 1877–1977; Atti del Congresso internazionale del centenario della nascita*, ed. Giovanni Dotoli (Fasano: Grafischena Fasano, 1978), 255.

31. "[E]ntre temps il [Hébertot] m'a mis en rélation avec Canudo qui avait donné un livret de ballet aux Suédois qui lui plaisait beaucoup. Canudo m'a montré les lettres échangées entre le théâtre et lui. On lui offre de monter son ballet si la musique est de moi. La malheur était qu'il en avait déjà parlé à un compositeur Italien Davico, mais il a pu s'arranger et c'est moi que fait la musique. J'ai vu de Maré le directeur des Suédois et Börlin le principal danseur et c'est maintenant une affaire décidée." Arthur Honegger to Oscar and Julie Honegger, Paris, 4 October 1921; collection Pascale Honegger, Geneva.

32. De Maré stated that the one-act ballet would be presented to the Société des Auteurs; 33% of the profits were to be Börlin's; 77% [*sic*—he must have meant 67%] were to be divided between Canudo and Honegger. De Maré to Canudo, Paris, 17 November 1921; Dansmuseet, Stockholm.

33. Canudo to de Maré, Paris (on the letterhead of CASA, the Club des amis du septième art), 26 November 1921; Dansmuseet, Stockholm.

34. Canudo, "Skating-Ring à Tabarin; Ballet-aux-Patins pour la musique de DAVICO," extract from *Mercure de France*, 15 May 1920, annotated in the margins by Jean Börlin; Dansmuseet, Stockholm.

35. See Honegger's datebook for 1921; collection Pascale Honegger, Geneva.

36. "J'ai vu Honneger *[sic]* à qui mes projets plaisent beaucoup. Il va se mettre au travail—dans un esprit assez ferme et net." Léger to de Maré, Paris, 21 November 1921; Dansmuseet, Stockholm.

37. "Je me suis embarqué dans ce ballet et cela m'absorbe beaucoup." Honegger to Oscar and Julie Honegger, Paris, 19 November 1921; collection Pascale Honegger, Geneva.

38. "Pour Borlin, qu'il ne s'inquiète pas. Le velours de lui et de sa danseuse donnera le relief désiré. . . . Je pense que Börlin voit aussi la chorégraphie dans cet esprit un peu cassant et brusque. Je le conçois avec un type jeune (son costume lui y prête) et plus fantasque que les autres, plus souple (opposition avec les autres groupes)." Léger to de Maré, 21 November 1921; Dansmuseet, Stockholm.

39. Fernand Léger, unpublished ms., "C'est Apollinaire qui m'a emmené voir Charlot"; Fernand Léger archives.

40. For an account of this see Rolf de Maré, *Les Ballets Suédois dans l'art contemporain*, 180.

41. Léger, "Le Spectacle: Lumière, couleur, image mobile, objet-spectacle," *Bulletin de l'effort moderne* 8 (1924): 5–9.

42. "Un peintre fut invité qui se mit à jouer un jeu nouveau sur le même thème. M. Fernand Léger, dont je ne me permetrai pas de juger le talent, ne me contradira pas si j'affirme que rien, dans sa technique de cubiste conscient et organisé, ne le désignait pour 'habiller' une oeuvre d'Honegger." Emile Vuillermoz, "Les Premiéres," *Excelsior*, 22 January 1922.

43. For Léger's reaction to *Skating Rink*, see Maurice Raynal, "Skating-Rink: Ballet de Fernand Léger," *L'Esprit nouveau* 17 (1922): 2113.

44. Léger and Cendrars began discussing the project before *Skating Rink* debuted. Cendrars wrote to Léger, "Tell de Maré . . . that I have the two subjects of the 'ballet nègres' ready; that with you I am ready to make a work of much greater breadth, very serious, very tough, very modern, that must be of one's time." ("Dis a de Maré . . . que j'ai tout prêt deux sujets de 'ballet nègres'; qu'avec toi je suis prêt à faire une oeuvre de plus longue haleine, très sérieuse, très dure, très moderne, qui fasse date.") Cendrars, unpublished letter to Léger, 29 October 1921; Fernand Léger archives.

45. Cendrars' book was originally to be three volumes. The first was to be a compilation of legends gleaned from materials available in France; the second based on foreign literature available at the British Museum; the third featuring stories of blacks in contemporary Africa and North and South America. Only volume one was completed. His source for the creation myth was Rev. P. H. Trilles, *Chez les Fang ou 15 années de séjour au Congo français*, Lille, France, 1912.

46. See Cendrars, "Séance nègre," unpublished ms., undated [c. 1922]; Archives Blaise Cendrars, Bibliothèque nationale suisse, Berne; also I. M. Kessler, *Les Ballets Suédois et les poètes français* (1920–1925), thèse du IIIe cycle, Université de Paris IV, 1982.

47. "Vous savez que nous pensons en faire une oeuvre importante extrêmement etudiée. Il devra être le seul ballet nègre possible dans le monde entier et être celui que restera comme typique du genre. . .Cela nécessite de nombreuse entraînes très minutieuse entre Cendrars, Börlin et moi." Léger, letter to de Maré, Paris, 12 September 1922; Dansmuseet, Stockholm.

48. See Léger, letters to de Maré, 12 September and 1 October, 1922; Dansmuseet, Stockholm.

49. "C'est une oeuvre importante, à laquelle Cendrars et moi devrons donner toutes nos soirées." Léger, letter to de Maré, 12 September 1922; Dansmuseet, Stockholm.

50. See Marie-Thérèse Audige, *Fernand Léger et le décor du théâtre; l'oeuvre dessinée*, diplôme, Ecole du Louvre, 1975, 59ff.

51. Manuscripts in the Cendrars archives trace the progression of the Cendrars-Léger collaboration: Cendrars, "Sypnosis d'un ballet nègre"; Cendrars, [Lighting instructions]; Cendrars, "Musique en rondeau [choreographic notes]"; Cendrars, "Ouverture [Musical instructions]"; Archives Miriam Cendrars, Paris. See also Ornella Volta, "Les 'Fêtes Nègres' de Blaise Cendrars," *Continent Cendrars* 6–7 (1991–92): 39–42.

52. Darius Milhaud, *Notes without Music*, trans. Donald Evans (London, 1952), 118. Milhaud visited Harlem in 1922 and returned to France with a substantial collection of Black Swan records.

53. Milhaud, *Notes without Music*, 127. On the sun and the moon, see interview with the late Mme Raymone Cendrars-Sausser, Lausanne, 3 December 1982.

54. "Ces grandes surfaces ocres, noires, blanches, rompent durement l'équilibre par ailleurs si remarquable dans la parution de Milhaud . . . palpitation des trompettes, le chant régulier du saxophone. . ." Léger to Florent Fels, cited in "Au Théâtre des Champs-Elysées: Ballets Suédois," *Les Nouvelles littéraires*, 10 November 1923.

55. "La scène moderne peut aller, si l'on veut, jusque-là, on possède les moyens de le faire. Le public suivra, il a suivi, l'épreuve est faite. Je veux rendre ici hommage à Rolf de Maré, directeur des ballets suédois, qui, le premier en France, a eu le courage d'accepter un spectacle où tout est machination, et jeux de lumière, où aucune silhouette humaine n'est en scène; à Jean Börlin et à sa troupe condamnée au rôle du décor mobile. . . . C'est en acceptant le ballet *Création du monde* (ballet nègre) qu'il a osé imposer au public pour la première fois une scène vraiment moderne, comme moyens techniques tout au moins. Le succès a récompensé son effort, le public l'a suivi franchement, directement." Léger, "Le Spectacle: Lumière, couleur, image mobile, objet-spectacle," *Bulletin de l'effort moderne* 8 (1924): 5–9.

56. For further details see Judi Freeman, "*Relâche* and *Entr'acte*," in *Francis Picabia 1879–1953*, exh. cat. (Edinburgh: Scottish National Gallery of Modern Art, 1988), 15–26, as well as the essay by William Camfield in this volume.

57. Fernand Léger, "The Ballet-Spectacle, the Object-Spectacle," in *Functions of Painting* (New York: The Viking Press, 1965), 72–3. First published in *Bulletin de l'effort moderne* (1925).

58. "[R]endu à l'art moderne d'exceptionnels services et values à chacun de nous de joies tellement grandes . . . à votre personne et à votre oeuvre un titre de plus à notre attachement et à notre reconnaissance." Rosenberg to de Maré, n.d. [1925, Friday night]; Dansmuseet, Stockholm.

Gerald Murphy, Cole Porter, and the Ballets Suédois Production of *Within the Quota*

Robert M. Murdock

The 1923 collaboration of painter Gerald Murphy and composer Cole Porter on an American "ballet-sketch" was a youthful effort, early in their respective careers, when they were both in their thirties. Though Porter had already written numerous songs and lyrics as a Yale undergraduate (including the well-known "Bull Dog"), and had composed *See America First* (produced in New York in 1916), his real celebrity as a composer and lyricist would not begin until 1928 with *Paris*, a musical that featured "Let's Do It, Let's Fall in Love."[1] Murphy, though an avid follower of the arts and ballet in Paris from his arrival in 1921, had just begun painting in 1922.

Much of the recent interest in Sara and Gerald Murphy is tied to the mystique of Paris and the French Riviera in the 1920s and the Murphys' friendship with such luminaries as Pablo Picasso, Scott and Zelda Fitzgerald, Ernest Hemingway, and John Dos Passos. As is often mentioned, the Murphys served as the models for the characters Dick and Nicole Diver in Fitzgerald's *Tender is the Night* (1934), though the Murphys did not recognize themselves in the novel, which was dedicated to them.[2]

Both Murphy and Porter represented the high style of the 1920s—the "good life" that often has been glamorized in books and documentaries on the period. Murphy was fond of quoting a Spanish proverb, "Living well is the best revenge," a motto that Porter, Harry Crosby, and other wealthy American expatriates shared. In his book of the same title Calvin Tomkins quotes Murphy's recollection of that time: "Every day was different. There was a tension and an excitement in the air that was almost physical. Always a new exhibition, or a recital of the music of Les Six, or a dadaist manifestation, or a costume ball in Montparnasse, or a première of a new play or ballet, or one of Étienne de Beaumont's fantastic 'Soirées de Paris' in Montmartre—and you'd go to each one and find everybody else there, too. There was such passionate interest in everything that was going on, and it seemed to engender activity."[3] This was the artistic climate in which *Within the Quota* was created.

The parallels in the lives of Murphy and Porter undoubtedly enhanced their collaboration and led to the friendship and correspondence that lasted the rest of their lives (both men died in October 1964). The background of their association dates back to 1911, when they were both Yale undergraduates (Murphy graduated in 1912, Porter the following year). When they first met they discovered a mutual enthusiasm for Gilbert and Sullivan. Murphy convinced the glee club

Fig. 5
GERALD MURPHY
Within the Quota, 1923, cat. no. 104.

Fig. 6
GERALD MURPHY
Costume design for the Millionairess in *Within the Quota*, 1923.

Fig. 7
GERALD MURPHY
Costume design for America's Sweetheart in *Within the Quota*, 1923, cat. no. 105.

popular images, showing the length of a ship compared to the height of a monument (e.g., the Pyramids, the Washington Monument, or a modern skyscraper) were used in steamship advertisements and as postcards from about 1910 through the 1930s. Murphy has altered the image so that the ship is seen with its bow downward rather than corresponding to the top of the building, as it would have been shown in a comparison postcard—perhaps alluding to the sinking of the *Titanic* eleven years earlier. The banded funnels and the masts fore and aft identify the ship as the *Leviathan*, which was the largest liner at the time (Fig. 4). Formerly the German liner *Vaterland*, the vessel had been seized in Hoboken in 1917, when the United States entered the First World War, and rechristened the *Leviathan*. It was used as a troop ship during the war and reconverted as a luxury liner after 1920. Her well-publicized maiden voyage to Europe was on 4 July 1923, when Murphy would have been developing his set design. Given the tabloid format and the immigration theme, it follows that Murphy would have chosen such a current, recognizable image for his backdrop, as well as one so loaded with irony: a vessel of German origin naturalized into an American icon. Since the *Leviathan* was operated by the United States Lines, she was subject to Prohibition, and no alcohol could be served on board, which ties in with Murphy's "Rum Raid" headline and the sober Reformer in the ballet.[16]

During 1923 Murphy also painted *Boatdeck* (now lost), a huge canvas that he exhibited at the Salon des Indépendants, where it became a cause célèbre among the jury and in the press. Murphy must have been working on the painting at the same time as his backdrop for *Within the Quota*; the two are related in both scale and iconography.[17]

Murphy's cover design for a program shows the Immigrant rendered in flat, cartoonish style over a collage of photographic images of New York buildings, steamship funnels, a trolley car, and an elevated railway (Fig. 5). Its dizzying jumble of diagonal axes and inverted images suggests Murphy's familiarity with contemporary dada and cubist collages (such as *Metropolis* by Paul Citroën), which he might have seen in Paris or in contemporary magazines. In a subtle reference to his own defection from New York and the family business Murphy incorporated the Mark Cross logo, visible between the legs of the figure.

The costume sketches for *Within the Quota* seem rather conventional as compared to the design of the backdrop, but they are consistent with the stereotypes portrayed: the Immigrant in an ill-fitting suit and hat; the Millionairess in full-length draped gown, cape, and tiara, and America's Sweetheart in a frilly dress and bonnet, looking like Little Bo-Peep (Figs. 6–7). There is some question as to the authorship of the sketches—whether they may have been executed by Sara rather than by Gerald, or whether the Murphys may have worked on them together. Stylistically it seems possible that the looser renderings of America's Sweetheart and the Millionairess were made by Sara, while the flatter, more schematic design for the Puritan was Gerald's (Fig. 8).[18]

Cole Porter's music reveals an analogous blend of contemporary, classical, and popular forms with the dominant rhythms and lilting melodies that would later mark his Broadway musicals. *Within the Quota* was his only symphonic composition. His wife, Linda, had been ambitious for him to become a serious composer, and his musical study at the Schola Cantorum in Paris as well as his association with Milhaud indicated that direction. As a contemporary critic remarked, Porter's score had more in common with Milhaud than with George Gershwin, whose *Rhapsody in Blue* would appear the following year.[19]

The ballet opens with a quiet passage, not unlike the beginning of Milhaud's *La Création du monde*. The haunting America's Sweetheart theme is introduced; it is repeated and developed in the final section. In the syncopated "Immigrants' Waltz," played by brasses, which follows, references to Igor Stravinsky's *Petrouchka* are heard.[20] With Stravinsky's prominence in the Paris music world at the time, and with so many of his compositions in the Ballets Russes repertory, it is not surprising that Porter would quote the older composer, either in homage or in jest.

Porter's composition also features ragtime, jazz and burlesque cadences, and sentimental, melodic themes, all woven together through the orchestration—strong brass passages alternating with strings and percussion—in an insistent, ongoing rhythm.

Porter's original score was for piano, and according

Fig. 8
GERALD MURPHY
Costume design for the Puritan in *Within the Quota*, 1923.

Fig. 9
MIGUEL COVARRUBIAS
Caricature of Jean Börlin in *Within the Quota*, 1923, cat. no. 17.

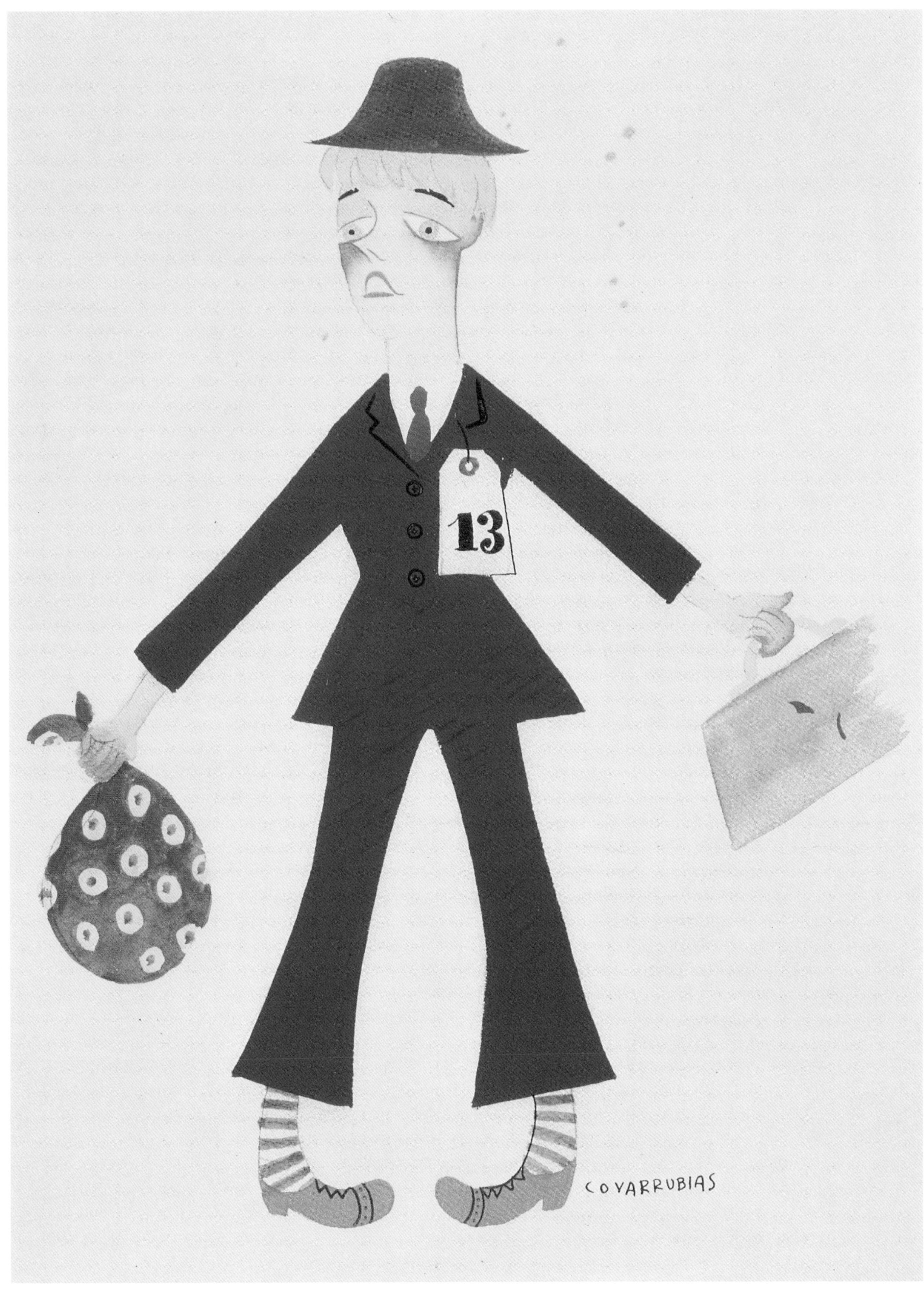
13
COVARRUBIAS

to a contemporary newspaper account, when he first presented it to Rolf de Maré, he recruited four pianists, from Venice, Lyons, Amiens, and Paris, to perform the work.[21] Whether truth or publicity stunt, this too may have been a reference to Stravinsky and the four pianos used on the set for *Les Noces*. Porter's piano score was then orchestrated by French composer Charles Koechlin, since Porter had done little orchestration at that point. The world premiere at the Théâtre des Champs-Elysées was conducted by Vladimir Golschmann, who also conducted the American premiere at the Century Theatre in New York on 26 November.[22]

Within the Quota was performed sixty-nine times and was critically acclaimed in Paris, New York, Philadelphia, and other American cities. The young Mexican artist Miguel Covarrubias, who had arrived in New York in 1923, apparently saw the performance there. His caricature of Jean Börlin as the Immigrant is in the exhibition (Fig. 9).[23]

Cole Porter, referring to *Within the Quota* as a "classical ballet," lamented the fact that, since the original music sheets were lost and he had no copies, "My one effort to be respectable must remain in limbo."[24] Though believed lost for years, an incomplete piano score for the ballet was discovered by historian Robert Kimball in the late 1960s among the papers that the composer had bequeathed to Yale. The Koechlin orchestration, though known to exist in the Dansmuseet in Stockholm, was not made available for performance until a few years ago.[25]

Within the Quota was revived as *Times Past* by the American Ballet Theater, New York, in 1970. By that year it must have indeed seemed like "times past," a nostalgic look back. But in original form it remains both a memorable collaboration and, as the first American jazz ballet, a historic milestone in the history of dance.

1. Robert Kimball, *The Complete Lyrics of Cole Porter* (New York: Knopf, 1983), introduction.

2. Calvin Tomkins, *Living Well is the Best Revenge* (New York: Signet, 1972), 12-13 [Original edition, New York: Viking Press, 1971].

3. Ibid., 33.

4. Robert Kimball, ed., *Cole* (New York: Holt, Rinehart, and Winston, 1971), 9-10. See also Tomkins, *Living Well*, 22.

5. Tomkins, *Living Well*, 15.

6. William C. Agee, "Gerald Murphy, Painter: Recent Discoveries, New Observations," *Arts* 59 (May 1985): 81-9. Agee discusses a newly located painting by Murphy, the *Villa America* sign.

7. Tomkins, *Living Well*, 36.

8. William Rubin, "The Pipes of Pan: Picasso's Aborted Love Song to Sara Murphy," *Artnews* 93 (May 1994): 138-47. See also Michael Kimmelman, "A Face in the Gallery of Picasso's Muses is Given a New Name," *New York Times*, 21 April 1994, which announced Rubin's article and stated his thesis. Kimmelman also cited the opinion of John Richardson, Picasso's biographer, that the final version of *Pipes of Pan* and its source, a homoerotic photograph by Baron Wilhelm von Gloeden, may allude to Murphy and Porter.

9. Tomkins, *Living Well*, 33.

10. Robert Orledge, "Cole Porter's Ballet *Within the Quota*," Yale University Library *Gazette* 50 (July 1975), 20.

11. Tomkins, *Living Well*, 41.

12. Bengt Häger, *Ballets Suédois* (New York: Abrams, 1990), 44. Häger quotes the scenario as described by *La Revue de France* at the time of the premiere. See also Kimball, *Cole*, 65-8; and William Rubin, *The Paintings of Gerald Murphy* (New York: The Museum of Modern Art, 1974), 24-9. While a number of sources refer to Murphy's scenario or "libretto" for *Within the Quota*, no such document appears to have survived.

13. The *New York Herald*, Paris edition, April-June 1923.

14. John Maxtone-Graham, *The Only Way to Cross* (New York: Collier Books, 1978), 11 [Original edition, New York: Macmillan, 1972].

15. Kimball, *Cole*, 57-8.

16. Maxtone-Graham, *The Only Way*, 137, 166.

17. Rubin, *The Paintings of Gerald Murphy*, 22. Rubin analyzed *Boatdeck* in relation to Demuth's *Paquebot Paris* but made the assumption that the liner depicted in Murphy's backdrop was also the *Paris*. Its identification as the *Leviathan* was made to this author by John Maxtone-Graham and confirmed by Frank Braynard, author of several volumes on the *Leviathan*.

18. Honoria Murphy Donnelly with Richard N. Billings, *Sara and Gerald: Villa America and After* (New York: Times Books, 1982), unnumbered page following 142. The caption for this illustration of costume sketches for *Within the Quota* reads "by Gerald, assisted by Sara." In a conversation with this author in October 1994 Mrs. Donnelly stated that her mother had done the sketches. William Rubin, in conversation, also acknowledged the question of authorship.

19. F. D. Perkins. *New York Tribune*, 29 November 1923. Quoted in Orledge, "Cole Porter's Ballet," 26.

20. Robert Kimball, "Cole Porter: Overtures and Ballet Music," liner notes, *Cole Porter Overtures, Ballet: Within the Quota* (EMI Classics compact disk, 1991). This performance by the London Sinfonietta, conducted by John McGlinn, uses the original Koechlin orchestration.

21. "Americans Supply a Ballet Suédois," *New York Herald*, Paris edition, 11 October 1923.

22. Orledge, "Cole Porter's Ballet," 21-2.

23. Covarrubias must have seen the ballet in New York, though it is not known whether he actually met Börlin. While there is no mention of Börlin or the Ballets Suédois in the recent biography of the artist (Adriana Williams, *Covarrubias* [Austin: University of Texas Press, 1994]) or in the exhibition catalogue of his caricatures (Washington, D.C.: National Portrait Gallery, 1985), Covarrubias was interested in jazz, theater, and dance, and he had already done some set designs (Williams, *Covarrubias*, 37-47). Since he had recently arrived in the United States himself, the Immigrant character may have appealed to him.

24. Cole Porter to Richard Hubler, quoted by Anna Kisselgoff, "Ballet by Cole Porter to Be Danced Here," *New York Times*, 5 May 1970.

25. Kimball, "Cole Porter," 7. Before the Koechlin orchestration became available, composer William Bolcom had reorchestrated the work after consulting with the Koechlin family, Darius Milhaud, and Vladimir Golschmann. He had been encouraged to undertake the project by the Cole Porter Trusts with the support of Gerald Murphy's daughter, Honoria Murphy Donnelly.

The Ballets Suédois and American Culture

Gail Levin

Several Americans interested in new forms of performance were attracted to the innovative reputation of Rolf de Maré, the young Swedish impresario of the Ballets Suédois, who commissioned ballets integrating the latest developments in music, poetry, drama, and film. An American tour resulted for the company, as well as the production of an American ballet and two little-known projects that were intended for the troupe but never completed. The history of the Ballets Suédois thus came to reflect some of the most significant intellectual forces in American culture of the early 1920s.

The Swedes were not chauvinistic, nor did they harbor nostalgia for their homeland. Enjoying artistic freedom at home, they went to Paris for cultural stimulation. Although their repertory included a few works with Swedish elements (such as sets by the painter Nils Dardel or the folk dances that inspired dancer-choreographer Jean Börlin), de Maré chose instead diverse collaborators, among them by 1923 the American team of Gerald Murphy and Cole Porter.

In early 1923 Murphy received a commission to create an "American" ballet through Fernand Léger, who was designing sets and costumes for the Ballets Suédois production *La Création du monde* (The Creation of the World) and needed a curtain raiser. Murphy was encouraged to find an American to compose a score in the American idiom. He chose Cole Porter, who had not yet achieved his popular success on Broadway. The two expatriates worked on the project for three weeks during the summer of 1923 in Porter's palazzo in Venice (Fig. 1). Jean Börlin was responsible for the choreography. They turned out an eighteen-minute piece, *Within the Quota*.

If the vogue for America in 1920s Paris moved Léger to turn to Murphy, the outcome must have been hugely satisfying. *Within the Quota* looks and sounds typically American. To be sure, Murphy had decided in September 1921 to escape to Paris and was living luxuriously in the tradition of wealthy American expatriates. He was motivated no doubt by dour assessments of the American scene like those of the critic Waldo Frank, who inveighed against America's "spiritual Puritan negation."[1] In the wake of the First World War Frank and other cultural commentators, like Matthew Josephson and Paul Rosenfeld, were crying out for the creation of a genuinely indigenous and modern culture in America; this rise of nationalist sentiment at home had echoes in Murphy's project.

Cinema took pride of place in Frank's assessment of American cultural inventiveness: "The true popular Theater of the American masses is . . . the Movie. Before

Fig. 5
Program cover for the 1923 American tour of the Ballets Suédois.

BALLETS
ALLETS
UEDOIS
SUEDOIS
F. LEGER

the Movie, the American masses had no theater." Frank went on to descry the need for further invention: "The whole world now has its cinemas. America alone has nothing else. America alone has nothing better."[2] Thus it hardly comes as a surprise that cinema figures not only in Murphy's *Within the Quota* but in the two unrealized American projects for the Ballets Suédois.

In November 1922 Matthew Josephson sounded another call for a new American culture in *Broom*, the dada magazine he coedited with fellow expatriate Harold Loeb. Josephson challenged Americans to create an indigenous art by drawing on popular culture; the artist needed to "plunge hardily into that effervescent revolving cacophonous milieu. . . where the Billposters enunciate their wisdom, the Cinemas transport us, the newspapers intone their gaudy jargon. . . and skyscrapers rise lyrically to the exotic rhythm of jazz bands."[3]

Josephson's smorgasbord of Americana reads like a manifesto for *Within the Quota*.[4] As a backdrop Murphy designed a giant front page in a parody of Hearstian yellow journalism (Fig. 2). Ears trumpet "EXTRA! FINAL EDITION" and mock banners flaunt sensationalist themes such as "Ex-Wife's Heart-Balm Love-Tangle" and "UNKNOWN BANKER BUYS ATLANTIC." Other juxtaposed headlines leave the eye uncertain whether to read across columns or simply down: "RUM RAID" could be followed by "LIQUOR BAN" or "ROMANCE." At top left an illustration compares an ocean liner tipped on its end to the Woolworth building. Built in 1913, it was in 1923 still the highest structure in the world, overshadowing the Eiffel Tower. As a symbol of America it had already attracted American modernist artists such as John Marin.

To one reporter Murphy explained that his set was "not Cubism, but its composition was inspired by Cubism,"[5] suggesting its relationship to Pablo Picasso's collages containing newsprint. Picasso was said to have returned the compliment, remarking of Murphy's set, "C'est beau, ça."[6] Murphy told a different story to American reporters, claiming that the set represented "a composite of 250 American newspapers that I have studied. . . The object is to get the quintessence of Americanism out of its newspapers."[7] The set design clearly shows that Murphy measured the American anatomy with an eye made all the sharper by the detachment of the expatriate.

Murphy's story line satirizes the impressions of a naive young Swedish immigrant to the United States, whose experiences range from victimization in New York (Fig. 3) to triumphant metamorphosis into a Hollywood

Fig. 1
Left to right: Gerald Murphy, Cole Porter, and the Porter's friend Sir Charles Mendl, The Lido, Venice, summer 1923.
Collection Honoria M. Donnelly, New York

movie star. French readers would see a parallel with Voltaire and the tribulations of Candide. The scene of arrival in New York may be reflected in the colossal painting *Boatdeck*, which Murphy exhibited in the Salon des Indépendants of 1924 and which, as William Rubin has suggested, may have been designed as an opening curtain for *Within the Quota*.[8] Murphy's scenario expands into a humorous picture of popular American stereotypes as observed through foreign eyes. Each of the characters and episodes draws on the American vernacular:

A millionairess, bedecked with immense strings of pearls, ensnares him; but a reformer frightens her away. Then a Colored Gentleman appears and does a vaudeville dance. He is driven away by a "dry agent" who immediately thereupon takes a nip from his private flask and disappears, to the immigrant's increasing astonishment. The Jazz Baby, who dances a shimmy in an enticing manner, is also quickly torn from him. A magnificent cowboy and a sheriff appear, bringing in the

Fig. 2
Within the Quota, Paris, 1923, cat. no. 228.

element of Western melodrama. At last the European is greeted and kissed by "America's Sweetheart"; and while this scene is being immortalized by a movie camera, the dancing of the couples present sweeps all the troubles away.[9]

Many of Murphy's character types and their costumes were borrowed directly from American cinema. Gerald and his wife Sara, who had both studied briefly with Natalia Gontcharova, together produced the costume designs, according to their daughter, Honoria.[10] America's Sweetheart appears dressed in tiers of ruffles, carrying a basket of flowers and looking a bit like Little Bo Peep. Murphy intended to evoke Mary Pickford's film image as a dimpled darling with golden curls, which earned her the moniker "America's Sweetheart." The Cowboy, sporting fur jodhpurs and a typical Texas ten-gallon hat, was modeled after popular western stars of the silent screen such as Fred Thomson and Tom Mix.

Murphy also drew upon other performing arts pivotal to American popular culture. The Colored Gentleman, with spats, a straw boater, and a cane, stepped right out of a vaudeville number. Murphy shared an admiration of vaudeville with some of his American avant-garde contemporaries, notably Man Ray and Marsden Hartley, whose essay "Vaudeville" appeared in 1921.[11]

Murphy personified the rhythm of jazz bands in the Jazzbaby, while Porter's score reiterated the allusion to the African American music that inspired so many contemporary American and European artists, including Albert Gleizes, Francis Picabia, and Man Ray. The Murphys themselves sang Negro folk songs and spirituals, which Gerald had collected for years, charming the French, especially the composer Eric Satie.[12] Jazzbaby attempts a sultry look, with a slinky gown slit up the side, a bracelet pushed above her elbow, and her cigarette thrust into the air (Fig. 4).

Porter's score also cleverly parodied the music playing in silent-movie theaters, where the orchestra

Fig. 3
Jean Börlin as the Immigrant in *Within the Quota*, New York, 1923, cat. no. 231.

Fig. 4
Jean Börlin as the Immigrant and Ebon Strandin as the Jazzbaby in *Within the Quota*, New York, 1923, cat. no. 229.

attempted to dominate but the piano always won out. Although Porter borrowed from jazz, he also drew from a variety of other sources, such as a Salvation Army chorale, a fox trot, a Swedish waltz, and the cacophony of New York taxi horns.

With his skyscraper, jazz, movie-style Wild West, vaudeville, and whiff of yellow press, Murphy was serving up in style what the Parisian avant-garde of the 1920s expected from America. "No one talked art in the group; it was simply not done. Vaudeville, the latest Argentinean tango, American jazz, skyscrapers, machinery, advertising methods — these were the new gods here," remembered poet Alfred Kreymborg (the original coeditor with Loeb of *Broom*).[13] Kreymborg described the French painter André Derain as "a magnificent figure of a man who wore a tremendous black sombrero which he removed with the majestic sweep of a cowboy in a wild-western movie,"[14] an image similar to Murphy's costume design for the cowboy of *Within the Quota*. The French enthusiasm for "a romantic America of cowboys, skyscrapers, and jazz" also impressed Frank when he reported the influence of American culture in France.[15]

Before the premiere on 25 October 1923 at the Théâtre des Champs-Elysées, Léger had de Maré change the order of performance lest such a lively curtain raiser steal the thunder from *La Création du monde*, which was also making its debut. As Léger suspected, critics loved the jazz elements of Porter's music. Gilbert Seldes had earlier characterized jazz as "the symbol, or the byword, for a great many elements in the spirit of the time — as far as America is concerned it is actually our characteristic expression."[16] He praised the production particularly for its music: "*Within the Quota* is actually an American ballet, the first to be produced by a foreign organization and the first in which popular American music exclusively has been used in connection with an American theme. Under the action lies the chief interest — that into eighteen minutes is 'collapsed' the small comedy of 'including the Scandinavian.'"[17]

Seldes identified the characters encountered by the immigrant as "the mythical heroes of contemporary American life, partly as the average European conceives them to be from acquaintance with our moving pictures, and partly as they are. The intention is satirical, the indicated method is exaggeration."[18] He admired Cole Porter, noting that "parody and comic exaggeration come naturally to him. In the cowboy, the 'colored gentleman,' and the finale, he has summed up nearly everything there is in the use of syncopation."[19] Seldes was also enthusiastic about Börlin's choreography, which he claimed was "made up of the characteristic steps of American dances, and the gestures of American everyday life." He dismissed Murphy's decor and costumes as being inconsequential except that they did not "distract from the story and the music."[20]

When the Ballets Suédois began its American tour in New York City in the autumn of 1923 (Fig. 5), it was Gilbert Seldes who was instrumental in recommending as a publicity agent the young literary critic Edmund Wilson, who remembered seeing the company not long after arriving in Paris on 20 June 1921: "Jean Cocteau took me to lunch and of course was gratified by my admiration. I had enormously enjoyed his *Mariés de la Tour Eiffel* (The Newlyweds on the Eiffel Tower), performed by the Swedish ballet, . . . with its ostrich and hunter in the Eiffel Tower and its general, a guest at the wedding, who is eaten by a lion. . . ."[21]

Wilson, who was then "very hard up," seems to have done his job well, for the invitation-only dress-rehearsal at the Century Theater on 25 November 1923 attracted

13

critics as influential as Frank; society patrons of the arts such as Gertrude Vanderbilt Whitney (the sculptor and future founder of the Whitney Museum), Otto Kahn, and the Damrosch sisters; writers Edna Ferber, Carl Van Vechten, and John Dos Passos; and noted artists George Bellows, William Glackens, Childe Hassam, and Boris Grigorieff, a Russian émigré painter.

The *New York Evening Star* reviewed the American debut with this headline: "Parisian Impressionism in Many Distended Moods, Including the Scandinavian; Imagery, Travesty and Eiffel Towerism." The company performed four works for the New York debut: *L'Homme et son désir* (Man and His Desire), based on a symbolist poem by Paul Claudel; *Skating Rink*, a one-act ballet based on a poem by Ricciotto Canudo with sets and costumes by Léger; *Les Mariés de la Tour Eiffel*, a farcical spectacle by Cocteau; and *Les Vierges folles* (The Foolish Virgins), a biblical parable recounted in the manner of a Swedish folktale.

America's mood of nationalism predisposed critics and audiences to appreciate evidence of particular traditional ethnic cultures. Thus the same critic who praised *Les Vierges folles* for its "Northern crispness," Swedish charm, and "tang of folk songs and hymns," panned Léger's modernist *Skating Rink* for its "scrambled paint," calling it grotesque and hoping that it would not "influence women's clothes."[22]

Murphy's *Within the Quota* was first performed in New York three days after the company's American debut. Deems Taylor, the critic in the *New York World*, pronounced it "at least amusing and colorful, blessedly brief, and spiced with the satire that consists in presenting slightly exaggerated facts," praising both Murphy's scenery and Porter's music.

The Ballets Suédois toured America, performing not only in East Coast metropolitan centers such as Washington, Philadelphia, and New York, but also in many other smaller cities and towns, through 1 March 1924. Conservative audiences caused de Maré to eliminate *La Création du monde* from the remaining performances because he believed it simply too modernist for the American public.

When the Ballets Suédois returned to New York for a Christmas-night performance it announced that "the 'ultra-modern' numbers in the repertory which aroused so much discussion. . . have been entirely eliminated and that the new program will include a number of the more traditional ballets which have been popularized by the organization in Europe."[23] *Within the Quota* was the only modernist ballet retained.[24] Murphy's piece was called "an ironical ballet sketch," and Murphy was said to have "availed himself of the privilege of an American to make good tempered fun of his own country."[25]

The success of *Within the Quota* encouraged other Americans to envision projects for the Ballet Suédois. One was conceived by none other than the company's American publicity agent, Edmund Wilson, who recalled, "I had the idea that it might be possible to induce Charlie Chaplin to perform in one of the pantomime ballets, and I convinced the impresario, Rolf de Maré, of the feasibility of this. He paid my expenses for a trip to California [in 1924] to try to persuade Chaplin."[26]

Wilson's esteem for Chaplin was widely shared. Frank had called him "our most significant and most authentic dramatic figure."[27] Since 1916 Léger too had admired the versatile American actor and, in 1920, he illustrated Ivan Goll's *Die Chaplinade*.[28] Four years later Léger asserted in an essay, "Le Ballet-Spectacle, l'objet-spectacle," that Chaplin was the film actor most able to employ the antiliterary, anti-individualistic potential of film.[29] Wilson may well have known Léger's drawings of Chaplin that appeared in *Broom* (Figs. 6–7). Unfortunately for Wilson, Chaplin declined to participate in the project, saying that he only performed in shows that he himself created.[30] Wilson concluded that Chaplin was "jealous of his independence. . . .[H]e is very unlikely to allow himself to be written for, directed, or even advised."[31]

Chronkhite's Clocks was the title of the ballet that Wilson had written for Chaplin. Wilson wrote to his friend the critic and poet John Peale Bishop on 15 January 1924, describing his creation as "a great super-ballet of New York for the Swedish Ballet" and explaining that it would include

> *a section of movie film in the middle, for which [Leo] Ornstein is composing the music and in which we hope to get Chaplin to act. It is positively the most titanic thing of the kind ever projected and will make the productions of Milhaud and Cocteau sound like folk-song recitals. It is written for Chaplin, a Negro comedian, and seventeen other characters, full orchestra, movie machine, typewriters, radio, phonograph, riveter, electromagnet, alarm clocks, telephone bells and jazz band.*[32]

The idea of using machines recalls both the inventive experimental music of Edgar Varése and the visual images of New York dada, particularly those in little magazines such as *291* and *The Soil*. Marcel Duchamp's recent experiments with moving images may have suggested "movie machines," while Picabia had already depicted an alarm clock in *291*. When Wilson met Cocteau in Paris he had letters of introduction from Frank Crowninshield, his editor at *Vanity Fair*, to Mme

Figs. 6–7
FERNAND LÉGER
Charlie Chaplin, 1922. Published in *Broom*, vol. 1, no. 3 (January, 1923).

Picabia and others.[33] Wilson's interest in dada, nowhere more apparent than in *Chronkhite's Clocks*, is also evident in his play *The Poet's Return*, with its conversations between the critics Rosenfeld and Josephson, and by the subsequent inclusion of Tristan Tzara's "Memoirs of Dadaism" in Wilson's influential 1931 book *Axel's Castle*.[34]

Wilson's characters include Mr. Chronkhite, who "has a time-clock dial for a face and time-clock indicators for hands; his shirt-front is a time-clock chart and he wears gun-metal clothes."[35] The office setting is in the "Bedlam Building." Other characters include "Cavan, The Can-Opener King," who sports "a flat beaked head like a can-opener blade," "O. J. Stuck," with "a head like the top of a glue-pot," and other equally absurd figures.[36] The pantomime pokes fun at new American technologies: the "Elevated Express" with "Electro-Pneumatic Sliding Doors" is supposed to offer "Increased Service" but instead jumps the track and "topples."[37] Despite the dadaist origins of his scenario, Wilson sought out the innovative set designer Robert Edmond Jones to create his sets instead of a dada artist such as Picabia or Duchamp.

Although Wilson failed to realize the production, he was nonetheless early to see the value of writing "a ballet on an American theme using authentic American material."[38] He admired Murphy's *Within the Quota*, claiming that it "had a certain finish and point" though it "scarcely pretended to be more than [a] trifle."[39]

At least one other American became involved in an unrealized idea for the Ballets Suédois: the expatriate American painter Morgan Russell. In early 1925 the poet Blaise Cendrars, who produced the scenario *La Création du monde*, wrote to Russell, encouraging him to develop the concept of a synchromist ballet.[40] Cendrars and Russell met in the south of France in 1917; Cendrars's poem "Ma danse" had appeared in 1914 on the same page as one of Russell's drawings in the review *Montjoie!*[41]

Synchromism was a style of colorful abstract painting, often with a figural basis, which Russell, together with a fellow expatriate American, Stanton Macdonald-Wright, had invented and promoted in Paris before the First

Fig. 8
Morgan Russell
Syncromy in Orange: To Form, 1913–14
Oil on canvas (135 x 121.5 cm)
Albright-Knox Art Gallery

World War (Fig. 8). The abstract quality of synchromism gave it international resonance, especially given certain resemblances to the work of the Parisian artists Sonia and Robert Delaunay.[42] A synchromist ballet could not have conveyed the same kind of pointedly American qualities as *Within the Quota* or Wilson's plans for a New York theme, even through synchromism was technically an American style, invented by expatriates living in Paris.

The notion of a synchromist ballet harmonized with Russell's interest in experimenting with ideas related to film. What he envisioned must have been a ballet of moving colored shapes similar to his unrealized idea for a kinetic light machine, which was to be a cinematic projection of abstract colored forms. Lacking funds for equipment, he produced studies for his machine in oil paint on tissue paper so that they could be illuminated from behind, as if projected. Cendrars's thoughtful advice to Russell on developing a synchromist ballet was:

forget the anecdotal aspect (. . . we can always think about it at the very last minute and then choose a subject which can be indicated by the dancer) but keep on with Synchromism, structure, the superhuman, the cosmic and by thinking of all this, it will all come together in your mind and some day soon you will find how to achieve all this technically.[43]

Since the Swedish company was on tour he advised Russell, "[y]ou have the time." Russell was enthusiastic about the project of collaborating with Cendrars, but his loyalties to Macdonald-Wright, his former partner in synchromism, caused him to hesitate. The old collaboration proved unobtainable, with Macdonald-Wright then living in southern California. Russell described Cendrars and his ballet proposal in a letter to his colleague:

His taste and work is very modern and he is one of the few who don't understand why I didn't persevere in painting Synchromies. . . . Of course, I've never considered a Synchromist ballet — but at once saw how it could be done and encouraged by his enthusiasm. Now, as you know — I don't wish to noisily resurrect Synchromism with you out of it, any more than you do, by leaving me out in [the] U.S. . . .[44]

As luck would have it, Börlin fell ill and de Maré consequently decided to disband the Ballets Suédois, making it impossible for either Wilson or Cendrars and Russell to accomplish their projects for the company. The realization of Russell's conception might have broken new ground for visual spectacle in dance. Although Wilson's plans certainly could have resulted in another American ballet, the premature demise of the company left *Within the Quota* to stand alone.

1. Waldo Frank, *Our America*, (New York: Boni and Liveright, 1919), 225.

2. Ibid., 214.

3. Matthew Josephson, "The Great American Billposter," *Broom* 3, November 1922, 305.

4. Elizabeth Hutton Turner, *American Artists in Paris, 1919-1929* (Ann Arbor: UMI Press, 1988), 138 and 141, attributes Murphy's interest in advertising and headlines to his friend John Dos Passos, but such preoccupations were then widespread.

5. William Rubin, *The Paintings of Gerald Murphy* (New York: The Museum of Modern Art, 1974), 16.

6. Calvin Tompkins, *Living Well Is the Best Revenge* (New York: E. P. Dutton, 1982), 40.

7. Rubin, *Murphy*, 29.

8. Ibid., 20.

9. Ibid., 24 and 28.

10. Author's interview with Honoria Murphy Donnelly, August 1992.

11. Marsden Hartley, "Vaudeville," in Hartley, *Adventures in the Arts* (New York: Boni and Liveright, 1921), 162-74.

12. Tompkins, *Living*, 28.

13. Alfred Kreymborg, *Troubadour: An Autobiography* (New York: Liveright, 1925), 366.

14. Ibid., 367.

15. Waldo Frank, *In the American Jungle: 1925-1936* (New York: Farrar and Rinehart, 1937).

16. Gilbert Seldes, "Toujours Jazz," *The Dial*, August 1923.

17. Gilbert Seldes, "Within the Quota," *Paris-Journal*, 1923.

18. Ibid.

19. Ibid.

20. Ibid.

21. Edmund Wilson, *The Twenties*, ed. Leon Edel (New York: Farrar, Straus and Giroux, 1975), 91.

22. Jean Henry, "'Swedish Ballet' Dancers at Century are Free from Mannerisms," *New York Evening Journal*, 26 November 1923.

23. "Swedish Ballet Here Again Christmas Night," *New York Telegraph*, 23 December 1923.

24. "More Exotic Beauty," *New York Evening Mail*, 27 December 1923.

25. "Swedish Ballet in Fine Program," *New York Evening Telegram* 27 December 1923.

26. Wilson, *The Twenties*, 153.

27. Frank, *Our America*, 214.

28. See Christopher Green, *Léger and the Avant-garde* (New Haven: Yale University Press, 1976), 248.

29. Ibid.

30. See Martin Green and John Swan, *The Triumph of Pierrot* (New York: Macmillan Publishing Company, 1986), 47.

31. Edmund Wilson, "The New Chaplin Comedy," reprinted in Wilson, *The American Earthquake* (New York: Farrar, Straus Giroux, 1958), 71.

32. Wilson, *The Twenties*, 153, excerpts Wilson to John Peale Bishop, 15 January 1924, Special Collections, Princeton University Libraries.

33. See Frank Crowninshield's memorandum of 13 June 1921 telling Wilson that he will meet Ezra Pound, Romain Rolland, and others through Mme Picabia; Edmund Wilson papers, Beinecke Library, Yale University. I am grateful to the Wilson biographer Lewis M. Dabney for his generous help with research on Wilson's connections to dada.

34. Edmund Wilson, *Axel's Castle: A Study in the Imaginative Literature of 1870-1930*, (New York: Charles Scribner's Sons, 1931), 304-12.

35. Edmund Wilson, *Chronkhite's Clocks*, in *Discordant Encounters* (New York: Albert and Charles Boni, 1926), 131-2.

36. Ibid., 139.

37. Ibid., 149.

38. Edmund Wilson, "American Jazz Ballet," in Wilson, *The American Earthquake*, 67.

39. Ibid.

40. Cendrars to Russell, 10 January 1925; see Gail Levin, "Blaise Cendrars and Morgan Russell: Chronicle of a Friendship," in *Dada/Surrealism* 9, 1979, 16.

41. *Montjoie!*, January-February 1914, an issue devoted to modern dance.

42. Gail Levin, *Synchromism and Color Abstraction, 1910-1925* (New York: George Braziller, 1978).

43. Cendrars to Russell, 10 January 1925, in Levin, "Blaise Cendrars and Morgan Russell," 16.

44. Russell to MacDonald-Wright, undated letter of 1925, in Levin, "Blaise Cendrars and Morgan Russell," 17.

Dada Experiment: Francis Picabia and the Creation of *Relâche*

William Camfield

The Ballets Suédois had a lot riding on *Relâche* (Cancelled), the principal new work for its 1924-25 season. Moreover, personal stakes existed for each member of the team: the director, Rolf de Maré, and his choreographer/dancer, Jean Börlin; scenarist and designer, Francis Picabia (Fig. 1); composer Erik Satie; and a young filmmaker, René Clair, hired to create a cinematic intermission. For Clair it was an unprecedented opportunity to launch his career. For de Maré and Börlin it was a matter both of pride and of survival in their competition with the Ballets Russes. De Maré had successfully challenged the vanguard status of Serge Diaghilev's company, but now there were financial concerns. In addition, for the 1923-24 season Diaghilev had replaced his traditional Russian repertory with ballets wholly produced by the Parisian avant-garde, in direct competition with the work of the Ballets Suédois.[1]

Conditions surrounding some of these Diaghilev ballets—*Les Biches*, *Les Fâcheux*, and *Le Train bleu*—had led to Satie's angry break with Jean Cocteau and the composers Georges Auric and Francis Poulenc.[2] At the same time, his kindred spirit, the former dadaist Francis Picabia, had declared war on the emerging surrealists and their leader, André Breton, who was one of Satie's least favorite persons. *Relâche* thus provided Picabia and Satie with a timely opportunity to integrate their iconoclastic talents in a production geared simultaneously to personal delight, dazzling chic Paris, and bedeviling their enemies of the day.

Relâche did not begin with all these personal agendas. It originated in the aftermath of *La Création du monde* (The Creation of the World), a very successful ballet produced in the fall of 1923 through the collaboration of Blaise Cendrars, Fernand Léger, and Darius Milhaud. Cendrars was asked to provide the scenario for a new work in conjunction with Satie, and they had already begun to work on it when Cendrars decided in January 1924 to accept an invitation to explore literary and business ventures in Brazil.[3] Satie quickly assumed the initiative. First he persuaded Cendrars to add Picabia to the list of candidates for designing the sets and costumes. Then, with Cendrars gone, he moved to secure Picabia's collaboration outright. Pierre de Massot, a young writer who idolized Picabia, conveyed Satie's invitation in a letter dated 22 January 1924. Picabia finally accepted, and de Massot replied:

> *I have seen Satie who is delighted with your yes. . . . Here is Cendrars' scenario, which is in no way final and on which you can embroider to your heart's delight. . . . Already the Cocteau crowd has got wind of it. Don't turn down the opportunity to dynamite Paris.*[4]

Fig. 2
FRANCIS PICABIA
Vive la vie. Published in *La Danse* (November-December 1924).

Première page

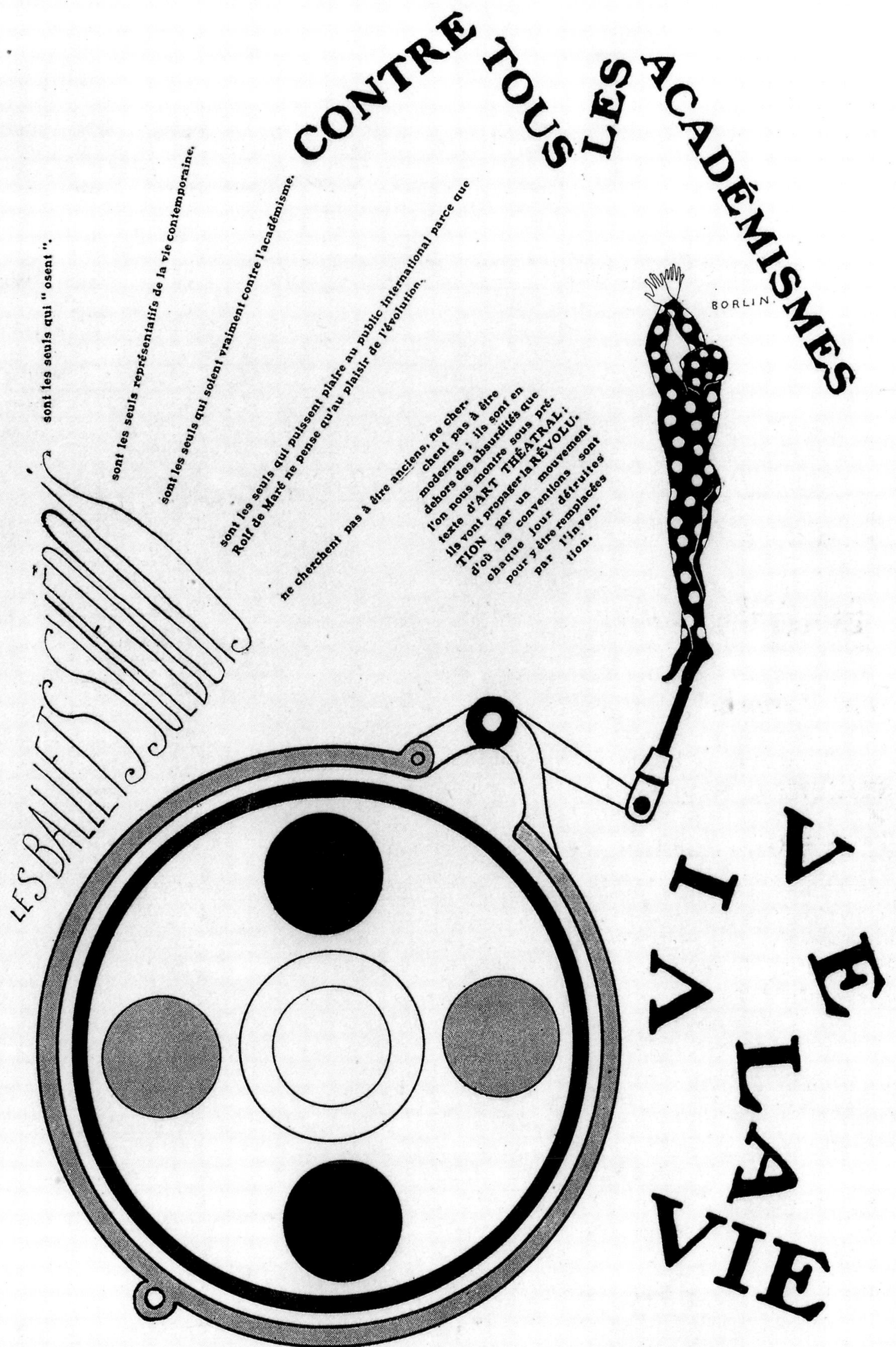

Fig. 1
FRANCIS PICABIA
Self-portrait, 1924, cat. no. 120.

Picabia's "embroidery" on the scenario and plans to "dynamite Paris" went apace from that moment onward. Traces of Cendrars's scenario, "Après dîner," remain in *Relâche*, but he never again figured in the production. Though he later grumbled that Picabia had usurped his place, Cendrars in effect forfeited any role in the ballet by not returning to Paris until early September.[5]

In March Satie wrote de Massot that *Picabia's* scenario (Satie's emphasis) was "trés chic,"[6] and in April—after de Maré's return from the costly United States tour of the company—Satie arranged a meeting which resulted in a new contract for the designer. Available documents do not record many details, but it is likely that by this date *Relâche* had acquired its title and basic structure, including plans for a filmed intermission entitled *Entr'acte* (Intermission).[7]

The exact date and conditions under which René Clair was selected to film *Entr'acte* are not documented, but scattered letters and other accounts attest to arduous and joyful labor by both Clair and Satie during the summer and fall. Clair wrote Picabia on 1 July that he had been working hard and was ready to present the finished film to him.[8] Picabia was delighted with what Clair had done with the meager scenario provided him; a week later de Maré began issuing his first press releases regarding the new ballet and film.[9]

Satie's letters document steady progress and great satisfaction in his work on the score for *Relâche*, followed by anxious labor over the music for *Entr'acte* until the last weeks before the premiere, scheduled for 27 November.[10] Two letters in particular reveal his ebullience. On 18 October he wrote to Paul Collaer: "In two days the orchestration of *Relâche* will be finished. . . . What a ballet! The premiere will be lively, believe me. The enemy forces—'this time'—will meet ours. We are mobilizing!"[11] A few days later he wrote Marcel Raval, editor of the magazine *Les Fueilles libre*: "It's *Relâche* that will give the signal for 'departure.' With *Relâche* we are

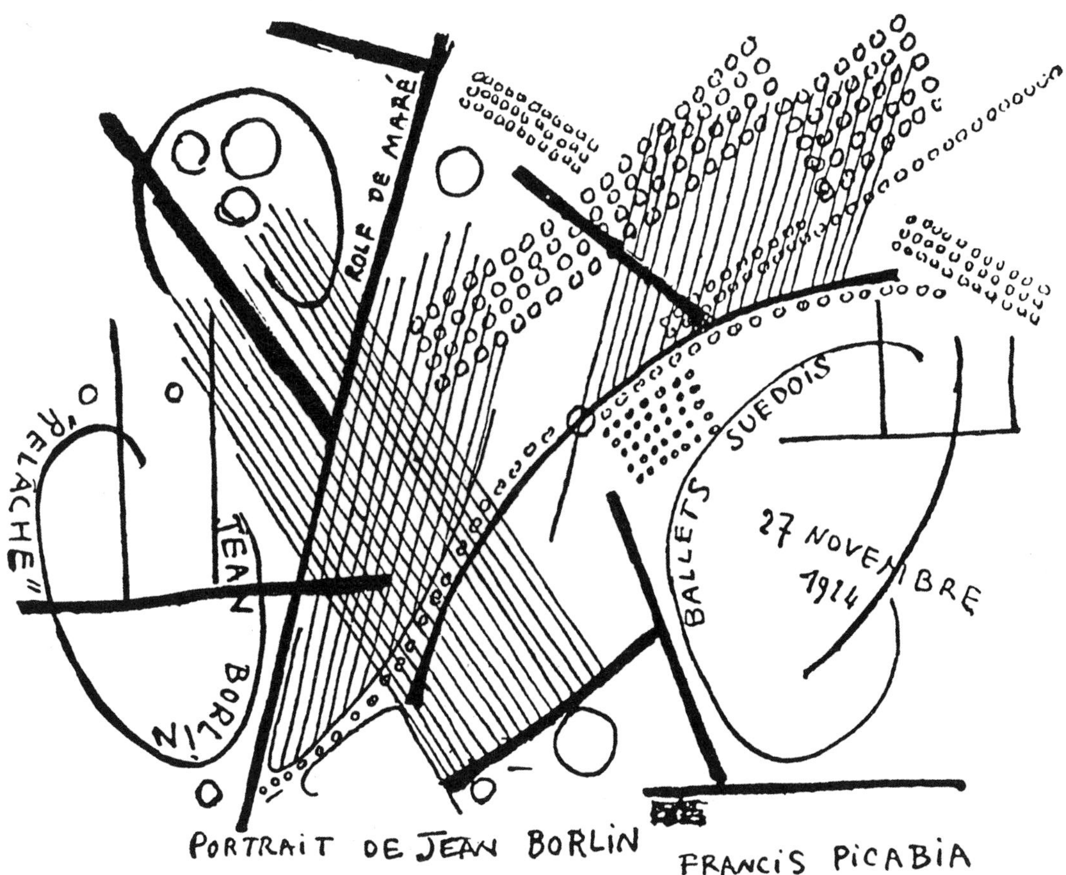

Fig. 3
FRANCIS PICABIA
Portrait de Jean Börlin, 1924.

entering into a new period. . . Picabia is cracking the egg, & we shall set out 'forward,' leaving the Cocteaus and other 'blinkered' people behind us."[12]

The attack against those "blinkered" people had been underway for months. Once Picabia had established the scenarios for *Relâche* around the end of April, he turned his attention to Breton and the emerging surrealist movement. Breton, after searching for a new direction in modern art and life that would supersede dada, finally brought surrealism into focus during the spring of 1924. As news of his concepts and plans for the movement surfaced, Picabia was among the first to take offense. His friendship with Breton, dating from the early days of dada, had always been uneasy, and he was simply unable to perceive in surrealism anything more than another of the pedantic experiments with which Breton had undermined dada. Picabia revived his dadaist magazine *391* and used it as a forum to ridicule Breton and his associates. Satie, given free reign there, took devastating potshots at Cocteau, Auric, and Poulenc.[13] Auric and the surrealists got their payback in June at the performance of *Mercure*, a ballet sponsored by Count Etienne de Beaumont with the collaboration of Picasso and Satie. The surrealists disrupted the second performance, shouting "Bravo Picasso" and "Down with Satie" until forcibly removed by guards.[14]

Those feuds simmered over the summer, then came to a rolling boil in the fall with Breton's publication of the "First Surrealist Manifesto" and an acerbic public exchange of articles, letters, and manifestoes.[15] Picabia contributed to those polemics, but he was far less interested in bashing Breton and surrealism than in promoting his own movement, instantanism, equating it with dada and proclaiming *Relâche* and *Entr'acte* as its primary manifestations.[16] De Maré and Picabia publicized instantanism, *Relâche*, and *Entr'acte* throughout November in advertisements and prominently placed articles illustrated with Picabia's machine portraits of his colleagues

(Fig 3). Self-mockery was a disarming weapon in much of that publicity. The general audience was advised to bring dark glasses and ear plugs, and the dadaists were invited to shout "Down with Satie! Down with Picabia! Long live La Nouvelle Revue française!"[17] Publicity culminated on the day of the premiere with Picabia's article, "Why I Wrote *Relâche*": "It is perpetual movement, life," he proclaimed; "it is the minute of happiness we all seek; it is light, richness, luxury, love far from prudish convictions, without morality for fools; without artistic refinement for snobs."[18]

At 9 p.m., with a crowd estimated at over 1,000 milling outside the doors of the Théâtre des Champs-Elysées, *Relâche* was indeed "relâche." The announced cause for cancellation of the performance was the illness of Jean Börlin.[19] Needless to say, many in the celebrity-studded crowd were skeptical. Picasso and Tzara considered it another of Picabia's dadaist pranks. Others saw the event as a beautiful outdoor ballet with all of Paris contributing—a crisp moonlit setting, the sounds of the taxis and the crowd, elegant women in jewels and furs, and a large assortment of the art and entertainment world—Marcel Duchamp, Constantin Brancusi, Man Ray and Kiki, Jacques Doucet, Sarah Rafaele, Marthe Chenal, Léger, and dozens of friends and enemies from the ranks of the surrealists and ex-dadaists.[20]

Relâche opened a week later to a packed house. Though it concluded a program that began with two earlier ballets, *Skating Rink* and *La Création du monde*, hardly a word about those pieces appeared in the reviews. Everyone had come for *Relâche*, and no one was disappointed. A strikingly designed program combined statements by the collaborators and drawings by Picabia (Figs. 2, 4–6). A brief filmed prologue by Clair showed Satie and Picabia descending in slow motion from above and firing a cannon from the roof of the Théâtre des Champs-Elysées into the audience and the city of Paris. As filmed by Clair that cannon shot literally turned the city upside down.[21]

The curtain then opened to a bare stage with a backdrop of 370 large metal reflecting disks, each equipped with an electric light; these were dimmed and brightened in coordination with the music, sometimes blinding the audience. A fashionably dressed woman (Edith Bonsdorff) sauntered onto the stage from her seat in the audience. She sat smoking while the orchestra played, then began to dance when the music ceased. A man in formal dress (Jean Börlin) entered in a paralytic's cart, but was quickly healed by the allure of Mlle Bonsdorff and accompanied her in the "Dance of the Revolving Doors" (Figs. 7–8). They were joined by eight males in formal attire from the audience (Figs. 9–11). As the men gathered around Mlle Bonsdorff, she stripped down to rose-colored tights, causing them to back off momentarily before coming together for the final dance of act 1. Throughout the act a chain-smoking fireman, decorated with the Legion of Honor, solemnly poured water from one bucket into another. Satie's music was correspondingly insouciant and fragmented, laced with allusions to popular, even bawdy, songs ("The Turnip Vendor" and "Have You Seen the Canteen Girl?").[22]

Following the cinematic intermission, the setting for the second act included signs or a backdrop (Fig. 12) with such provocative inscriptions as "Erik Satie is the greatest musician in the world" and "If you are not satisfied, whistles are on sale in the box office for two coins."[23] The second act was essentially a reversal of the sequence of act 1. The male dancers entered first in formal dress, followed by Mlle Bonsdorff, still in her pink tights but carried in on a stretcher. She proceeded to dress herself while the male dancers stripped down to white tights decorated with big spots suggesting clown costumes (Figs. 13–14). According to one critic the men began to dance joyfully around the ballerina but then danced with disdain around a classical statuette that temporarily replaced her.[24] The fireman continued to smoke and pour water. While the male dancers returned to their seats in the auditorium, the ballerina deposited their formal suits in a wheelbarrow and dumped them in a corner. She then tossed her crown of orange blossoms to one of the male dancers, who placed it on the head of the popular singer Marthe Chenal. As Mlle Bonsdorff resumed her seat in the audience a white curtain descended, and another ballerina concluded the performance by dancing and miming the words to Satie's music for "The Dog's Tail." During the curtain call Picabia and Satie, clad in fur and jewels, drove onstage in a midget Citroën to an ovation that astounded most critics.

For some observers *Relâche* was absolute nonsense, but as reconstructed here from contemporary accounts the ballet abounds with the spirit of Picabia's art: his audience-provoking inversion of the expected, such as the injection of music-hall slapstick into "serious" ballet; the ridicule of authority in the figure of the smoking fireman, a decorated hypocrite engaged in useless activity (a symbol of the academy); a disarming self-mockery, as in the selling of whistles; the power of sexual attraction; and disdain for the past and the history of art as represented by the classical statuette.

Judging from the lively audience reaction Picabia's

23
19
24
LE
BALLET
G
A
N
de LA MER GLACIALE

Fig. 2
GÖSTA ADRIAN-NILSSON [GAN]
(Lund, Sweden 1884–1965 Stockholm, Sweden)
Costume design for the Eskimo Princess in *La Mer glaciale*, 1923
Graphite and watercolor on paper, 35.3 x 24.4 cm
Nationalmuseum, Stockholm

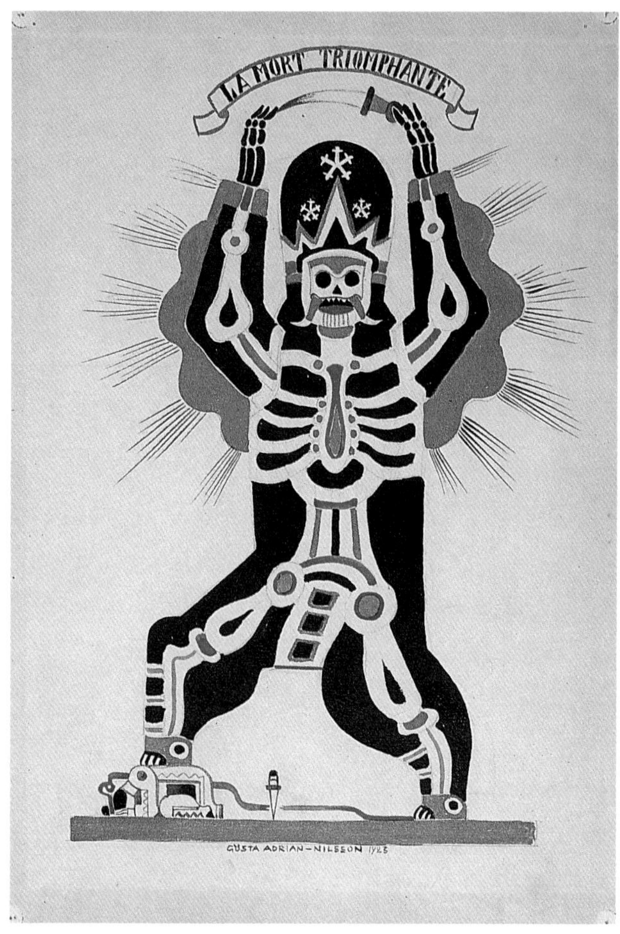

Fig. 3
GÖSTA ADRIAN-NILSSON [GAN]
(Lund, Sweden 1884–1965 Stockholm, Sweden)
"La Mer glaciale": La Mort triomphante, 1923
Graphite, watercolor, and gold paint on paper, 35.3 x 24.2 cm
Nationalmuseum, Stockholm

The Paris stay of Swedish pioneer modern artist Gösta Adrian-Nilsson [GAN] coincides with that of the Ballets Suédois. GAN was particularly interested in radical expression in the art of ballet and made pioneering suggestions for stage designs and costumes for several ballet productions. He shared this interest with Fernand Léger, the French cubist whose work he valued most.

In July of 1920, shortly after arriving in Paris, GAN contacted Léger and was very well received by him.[5] He was never a pupil of Léger's as were other Swedish artists arriving later; instead he was treated as an equal and a colleague. On one occasion the two artists even exchanged works of art.[6] GAN had been inspired by Léger as early as 1919, but he was never an imitator. In his view, influences from different artists and cultures intersected at all times. He was attracted to new artistic ideas with the instinct of a divining rod, as he was, for example, to the collages of Max Ernst, which he saw at an exhibit in May of 1921.[7]

GAN encountered the European art scene at the right time on two different occasions: in Berlin in 1913 and in Paris in 1920. During the 1910s he had developed his own highly personal synthesis of German-Russian expressionism, futurism, and cubism.[8] Movement in an image, based on principles of dynamic composition, interested him intensely, and this later became the cause of a certain amount of conflict with Léger.[9] GAN's strong interest in film and modern ballet was no accident. He detested naturalistic representation but was drawn to pantomime and expressive movement. He was an admirer of Charlie Chaplin, as was Léger, who used a Chaplinesque character in his film *Ballet mécanique* (1924).

Enthusiastically and with a remarkably keen eye for what was new, GAN saw performances at the Théâtre des Champs-Elysées by both the Ballets Russes and the Ballets Suédois. He was present at the revival of Igor Stravinsky's *Le Sacre du printemps* in Paris in December 1920, which again caused a tumult in the audience.[10] He also saw the Ballets Russes productions of *Parade* and *Le Tricorne*, with stage sets by Pablo Picasso. In June of 1921, after having seen the performance by the Ballets Suédois of *L'Homme et son désir* (Man and His Desire) with music by Darius Milhaud, and *Les Mariés de la Tour Eiffel* (The Newlyweds on the Eiffel Tower) with music by Arthur Honegger and others and a libretto by Jean Cocteau, GAN recorded rapturously in his diary: "It was like a dream—like something fantastical, taking place in a world other than that which heretofore had been shown on a stage—it was *fun*, as much fun as if one were a child playing with tin soldiers."[11]

In Paris GAN initially socialized more with musicians than with artists. He first became acquainted with Viking Dahl, who composed the music to the Ballets Suédois production of *Maison des fous* (Madhouse), with Nils Dardel's famous stage sets. GAN himself had made sketches for the ballet as early as July 1920,[12] possibly after discussing the matter with Dahl. After the premiere in November he arranged a reception for the prima ballerina of the company, Jenny Hasselquist, whom he knew from his time in Stockholm.[13]

In August 1920, when he lived on boulevard de la Tour-Maubourg, GAN became acquainted with Pergament, who also lived there. Pergament was so enchanted with GAN's painting *The Dream of Samoa* that he bought it immediately and composed a musical poem for it.[14] Through Pergament GAN quickly became part of a circle of musicians and composers that also included Matti and David Rubinstein (Pergament's other stepbrother) and Gösta Nystroem. "The Musicians," as GAN called them, rented a villa in Meudon, southwest of Paris, where GAN was a frequent guest during the winter of 1920–21. Inspired by his new friends, he experimented with a kind of musical notation in several colors many years before other artists were involved in the pictography of notation.[15]

Influenced by Stravinsky and in close collaboration with GAN, Pergament composed the music for an avant-garde ballet entitled *Krelantems and Eldeling*, with the principal female role intended for Hasselquist. While Pergament composed, first in Cannes during the spring of 1921 and later in Berlin, GAN was in Paris working on sketches for the sets and costumes. The progress of the project can be followed through letters from GAN to Pergament during the next two years. Regretfully, *Krelantems and Eldeling* was the only ballet produced of those for which GAN made sketches. It did not have its first performance until March 1928 at the Royal Opera in Stockholm, and by then GAN's interest in ballet was a finished chapter.[16]

GAN also developed an interesting collaboration with the composer Nystroem. Through his marriage in 1921 to Gladys Heyman, a sculptor from Gothenburg, Nystroem became well off financially and was able to help his impoverished namesake. It was Nystroem who made sure that GAN's important pamphlet, *The Divine Geometry*, was printed in Helsinki in 1922. After the Nystroems returned to Paris the same year, GAN was a frequent guest at their home on boulevard Péreire. During this period GAN and Nystroem collaborated on various ballet projects, among them *La Mer glaciale* (The Ballet of the Arctic Ocean) and *Söderhavsbaletten* (The Ballet of the Pacific).[17]

Without doubt *La Mer glaciale* was the most fully developed of these projects. In a radio interview shortly before his death Nystroem explained that the inspiration for the music came from a trip to the Arctic Ocean with Roald Amundsen in the early '20s.[18] Nystroem, who was a good friend of de Maré, managed to interest him in the project. "The project fell through because de Maré's premier dancer and choreographer, Jean Börlin, thought it was impossible to dance in the cubist-inspired costumes. A compromise with GAN was impossible, although I think that Börlin probably was right," Nystroem wrote in his autobiography many years later.[19] It is also possible that GAN's choleric temper was a hindrance in the efforts to interest de Maré in the project. Thora Dardel recalled an occasion during this period when she and Nils Dardel were invited to dinner at the Nystroems'. GAN had been given the honor of sitting next to the hostess at the dinner table. De Maré was also present, and it is likely that the Nystroems wanted to bring him together with GAN to discuss *La Mer glaciale*. Suddenly, however, GAN rose from the dinner table, annoyed by a remark by Gladys Nystroem, and simply marched off. Even if the threshold of tolerance was high in the Paris of the '20s, such behavior naturally attracted embarrassing attention. (It was with a slightly dizzy feeling that I listened in 1994 to 95-year-old Thora Dardel describe this episode, from more than seventy years before, as if it had happened yesterday. She died less than a year later, in March 1995.)[20]

The promising experimental collaboration between GAN and Gösta Nystroem was interrupted and never led to a performed ballet. After *La Mer glaciale* was abandoned Nystroem reworked the composition into a symphonic poem in 1924, *Ishavet* (The Arctic Ocean), first performed in 1927 in Stockholm and the following year in Gothenburg.[21] The importance to Nystroem of the collaboration is clear from a December 1926 letter he sent to GAN: "It would please me if you could come

G.A-N

Fig. 4
GÖSTA ADRIAN-NILSSON [GAN]
(Lund, Sweden 1884–1965 Stockholm, Sweden)
Costume design for two Eskimos in *La Mer glaciale*, 1923
Graphite and watercolor on paper, 35.3 x 24.4 cm
Nationalmuseum, Stockholm

Fig. 5
FERNAND LÉGER
Figure study for *La Création du monde*, 1923, cat. no. 95.

and listen, as you were the only one who was informed about it and who to an extent inspired me with your Eskimo drawings and your enthusiasm."[22]

While working on his exotic ballet projects GAN spent much time at the ethnographic museum in the old Trocadéro palace. There were extensive collections of art from Africa and Oceania at the museum but few objects from the still relatively unknown Inuit culture. GAN's references to Iniut culture in the sketches for *La Mer glaciale* are of a general character, consisting of igloos, Arctic animals, harpoons, paddles, and skis. To be sure, his aim was not ethnographic authenticity; instead he gave free play to his imagination, based on impressions he absorbed at the museum. He may also have consulted books. (When I interviewed Pierre Robbe, the curator at Musée de l'Homme and an expert on Inuit culture, he repeatedly mentioned that the "Eskimos" in GAN's sketches lacked ethnographic authenticity. He expressed his admiration for the beauty and immediacy of GAN's ballet sketches and stressed the right of the artist to freely interpret his sources of inspiration. An example of GAN's interpretive imagination can be seen in the expressive sketches for five animal masks for *La Mer glaciale*, plus a totemlike figure of obscure origin and meaning. GAN's masks suggest bears, a whale, a walrus, and a seal, but Robbe informed me that the Inuit only use bird masks.[23] Another example that reappears in several sketches are the spears that his Eskimos carry, which look more like the lances in Paolo Uccello's battle painting in the Musée du Louvre than real harpoons.)[24]

On 16 November 1923 GAN noted in his diary that he had finished the sketches for *La Mer glaciale*.[25] He spelled the word "ballet" as "ballett"—a combination of Swedish and French spelling—on the brown cardboard binder and on the flyleaf, which includes a dedication to Gösta Nystroem.[26] The same month, Nystroem received the complete portfolio as a gift from GAN, with the exception of two sketches that had already been acquired by the Gothenburg Museum of Art.[27] As far as is known, GAN's work for *La Mer glaciale* consists of thirty-six sketches for costumes and stage sets, the brown cover, the flyleaf with the dedication to Nystroem, and a sketch for a poster or program cover in green, black, and white, making a total of thirty-nine items. On this latter sketch GAN has written "LE BALLET de LA MER GLACIALE" and has added 1923–24 (Fig. 1). The sketch shows a fully-rigged ship above a globe, with symbols of the zodiac just beneath the equator. The ship and the globe are inside a triangle, with GAN's initials outside its points. There are other significant details: waveforms and a star above the globe's north pole, and a larger star

G.A-N.
Ishavsbaletten
Djurmask.

Fig. 6
GÖSTA ADRIAN-NILSSON [GAN]
(Lund, Sweden 1884–1965 Stockholm, Sweden)
Costume design for a Polar Bear in *La Mer glaciale*, 1923
Graphite and watercolor on paper, 31.3 x 24.1 cm
Nationalmuseum, Stockholm

Fig. 7
FERNAND LÉGER
Costume design for a godlike figure in *La Création du monde*, 1923, cat. no. 83.

inside a pentagram placed above the great mast of the ship. Four pointed triangles radiate diagonally upward from the globe, perhaps symbolizing the northern lights.

Fortunately, the suite of sketches for *La Mer glaciale* was not split up (except for the two sheets at the Gothenburg Museum of Art) as were the sketches for *Krelantems and Eldeling*. Gösta Nystroem kept the suite unbroken until his death in 1966. Eventually it was purchased as a whole in 1980 by the Swedish National Museum of Fine Arts for 96,500 Swedish crowns (then approximately 22,800 U.S. dollars). These sketches thus offer the best opportunity for study of GAN's interest in ballet from 1921 through 1923. These years represent a very important interlude in his artistry. In examining these sketches today I am struck by how remarkably fresh and well preserved they are. Clearly they have fared well, stored out of daylight all these years, as the colors still glow with undiminished brilliance.[28] GAN moves from watercolor to black ink, from drafts for curtains and stage sets to sketches for costumes and masks. His love for the sea and his sense of romantic exoticism have given his imagination ample space.

Regretfully, no libretto or story synopsis has been preserved. Lacking a story line, we might try to imagine how the drama develops. A hypothetical structure might be this: *La Mer glaciale* takes place in a small village of igloos surrounded by snow, ice, water, stars, the northern lights, and the eternal darkness of the polar night. The main thread is a crime of passion, particularly resonant in the ice-cold northern expanses. GAN's obsession with the sea takes the shape of a French sailor, the only survivor of a shipwreck in the Arctic Ocean. The sailor is thrown ashore and rescued by Eskimos, who gradually invite him into their lives and rites. He meets and falls in love with the daughter of the Eskimo chief (Fig. 2). She, however, is already engaged to a young Eskimo and is torn between her old and new love. This story is interspersed with hunting scenes and ritual dances of a magical character.

The drama ends with a life-and-death duel between the sailor and the Eskimo, each with a knife in his hand, bound together by a belt until one is victorious, as in Old Norse tales. Although the sailor is the victor in the bloody fight, there is no happy ending. In the magnificent final scene the brokenhearted Eskimo princess lies prostrate before a terrifying skeleton raising a bloody dagger above her crown of ice crystals (Fig. 3). This is *la mort triomphante*, death triumphant, of the *grand finale* to *La Mer glaciale*. Presumably the ballet culminates in a cascade of color and dancers in orgiastic movements. Seeing GAN's sketches for the immense animal masks, one can understand the reluctance Börlin felt about dancing in them.[29] According to Björn Springfeldt this Arctic love drama presents "an exotic and harmonious world, shattered in the meeting with *the foreign*."[30] The sailor, in European clothes and with a blue tattoo in the form of an anchor cross, is a Nietzschean superman, who destroys the closed, "primitive" Eskimo culture that he intrudes upon. *La Mer glaciale* may indeed contain an indirect but intentional critique of civilization. GAN's sympathies with Western culture were definitely not strong at this time, and interest among avant-garde artists in so-called primitive art and culture had been great since the beginning of the century.

It is interesting to note that Léger's *ballet nègre, La Création du monde* (The Creation of the World), presented by the Ballets Suédois, had its premiere at the Théâtre des Champs-Elysées in the same month that GAN completed his sketches for *La Mer glaciale.*[31] However, GAN and Léger differed greatly in their interest in primitive art. Like most cubists Léger was interested mostly in African art, while GAN was inspired by American Indian culture, with its colorful costumes and sweeping plumage. It is no coincidence that his Eskimos resemble American Indians more than Inuits, and this is only partly due to his lack of knowledge about Inuit culture. GAN felt a romantic, boyish admiration for the pride and indomitable will of the American Indians, and he returned at irregular intervals to Indian motifs in his pictures.[32] The knives and the bows in *La Mer glaciale* are of this type. GAN by no means avoided bloody and aggressive images, even though the violence is very stylized. The stronger individual triumphs, but in the end death still conquers all.

Léger's stage designs for *La Création du monde* are filled with magnificent, primitive power based on strong and simple forms and colors. GAN's sketches, on the other hand, contain a joyful delight in a wealth of decorative and ornamental details, combined with a veiled symbolism foreign to Léger (Figs. 4–7). GAN tells a secretive story with the refinement of an oriental miniature, partially disguised in cubistic dress. It is likely that he was more inspired by his visits to the Trocadéro Museum in his geometric designs for the Eskimo costumes than by the cubism of his day. The geometric shapes recur in combinations and with a frequency that cannot be coincidental. It is the author of *The Divine Geometry* that speaks through these exquisitely beautiful sketches, but the geometry is present as much in the hidden structure and balance of the images as in the ornamentation of the costumes. The energy of the dancers is obvious in these sketches, where the artist seems to have frozen their movements for a moment. GAN himself said that the most important aspect of his art was movement.[33] From this point of view it must have seemed like a dream come true to work on the stage designs for a ballet.

A detailed analysis of GAN's ballet sketches would probably reveal hidden meanings and make the contents of the drama more explicit. Such an investigation is beyond the scope of this essay, as my primary aim is to place GAN's ballet sketches in the context of their time. *La Mer glaciale* could have been in the class of Léger's famous ballets had the two Göstas, Adrian-Nilsson and Nystroem, been given the opportunity to bring their collaboration to completion. It could have become a landmark in the short but eventful history of the Ballets Suédois.

After more than seventy years GAN's sketches for *La Mer glaciale* shine with undiminished power, beauty, and creative joy. In Nils Lindgren's 1949 book about GAN the title of one chapter is "Ballet Interlude."[34] The more I delve into GAN's interest in ballet, the more I am struck by the central place that this "ballet interlude" takes in his artistry during the twenties, in spite of the fact that there were minimal concrete results. The sketches for *Krelantems and Eldeling* in 1921 prepare the way for *La Mer glaciale* in 1923. The development continues through GAN's final powerful artistic development during the Paris years, the Gothic book illustrations of his *Folk Songs* of 1924–25.[35] These in turn open wide the door to the new phase GAN entered when he returned to Lund, his home in Sweden, in May of 1925.

1. Gösta Nystroem, *Alt jag minns är lust och ljus* (All I Remember Is Joy and Light) (Stockholm, 1968), 69.

2. Ibid., 71f.

3. Bengt Häger, trans. and rev., *Rolf de Marés svenska balett* (Stockholm, 1947), 24, from the French by Rolf de Maré, *Les Ballets Suédois dans l'art contemporain* (Paris: Editions du Trianon, 1931

4. See Bengt Häger, *Ballets Suédois* (Paris and Stockholm, 1949).

5. GAN's diary no. 13, the GAN Archive, University Library, Lund, Sweden. All GAN's diaries have been preserved in this archive. The first meeting with Léger took place on 14 July 1920.

6. GAN's diary no. 16, 2 January 1922. GAN received an abstract watercolor by Léger in exchange for a cubist sculpture.

7. GAN's diary no. 15, 15 May 1921. Although GAN does not mention Max Ernst by name, it is clear from the circumstances that it was the Max Ernst exhibit of dadaist collages in Paris in May 1921 that he saw.

8. See J.T. Alstrand, *GAN: Gösta Adrian-Nilsson: Modernist-pionjären från Lund 1884-1920* (GAN: Gösta Adrian-Nilsson: A Pioneer of Modernism from Lund 1884-1920) (Lund, 1985).

9. Because of GAN's younger colleague and friend, artist Erik Olson (1901-1986), GAN and his artist friend from Lund, Wiwen Nilsson (1897-1974) considered Léger to be too "static" while GAN, on the contrary, represented "dynamism" in his art. This statement was repeated on several occasions by Erik Olson in personal interviews and in letters to the author.

10. Nystroem, *Alt jag minns är lust och ljus*, 9.

11. GAN's diary no. 15, 21 June 1921.

12. GAN's diary no. 13, 27 July 1920.

13. GAN's diary no. 14, 10 November 1920.

14. GAN's diary no. 13, 11 August 1920. See also Nils Lindgren, *Gösta Adrian-Nilsson* (Halmstad, 1949), 110ff.

15. Concerning GAN's relations with "The Musicians," see GAN's diaries nos. 13-15, 1920-1921. See also Lindgren, *Gösta Adrian-Nilsson.*

16. In his monograph on GAN from 1949 (see note 14), Nils Lindgren devotes one chapter called "Ballet Interlude" to GAN's ballet sketches. The emphasis is on *Krelantems and Eldeling. La Mer glaciale* is hardly touched upon. The first study of this central work of GAN's is my essay "GAN och balletkonsten" (GAN and the Art of Ballet) in *GAN: Gösta Adrian-Nilsson: La Mer Glaciale: Ishavsbaletten 1923* (GAN: Gösta Adrian-Nilsson: La Mer Glaciale: The Ballet of the Arctic Ocean 1923), preface by Björn Springfeldt, exh. cat. (Malmö Konsthall, 1987).

17. In his diaries from 1921-1923 GAN often refers to his friendship with Gösta and Gladys Nystroem. Lindgren, *Gösta Adrian-Nilsson,* has published extracts of letters from GAN to Gösta Nystroem. It was thanks to the intervention of Nystroem that GAN could publish his famous (in Swedish art) pamphlet *Den gudomliga geometrien* (The Divine Geometry) (Helsinki, 1922), which he had written already in May 1921.

18. Swedish Radio, 7 May 1966, interview with Gösta Nystroem.

19. Nystroem, *Alt Jag minns är lust och ljus,* 86f. One of GAN's sketches for *La Mer glaciale* was reproduced in Nystroem's book, 85.

20. Interview with Thora Dardel, Stockholm, 19 May 1994. See also Thora Dardel, *Jag for till Paris* (I Went to Paris) (Stockholm, 1941), rprt. 1994, concerning the Parisian artistic environment of the '20s.

21. First performance on 2 November 1927, in Stockholm, second on 15 February 1928, in Gothenburg. After another 36 years *Ishavet* (The Arctic Ocean) was performed anew in Gothenburg, in 1964, and two years later by the Swedish Radio Symphony Orchestra in a broadcast of 7 May 1966, when Nystroem also was interviewed (see note 18). After the rediscovery of the original score in Uppsala in the '70s, *Ishavet* was finally reworked into a ballet *[sic]* and first performed as such at the Royal Theater in Stockholm in 1977, more than ten years after the death of Nystroem. See *Isahavet,* program for the Ballet at the Royal Theater, Stockholm, 1977.

22. Letter from Gösta Nystroem to GAN, December 1926, GAN Archive, Lund, Sweden.

23. Interview with Pierre Robbe, curator at the Musée de L'Homme, Department of Ethnology, Paris, 27 January 1994.

24. GAN was—like Léger—a great admirer of the "cubism" in Paolo Uccello's famous battle painting from the 15th century and used it as a source of inspiration in some of his works from this period.

25. GAN's diary no. 18, 16 November 1923.

26. National Museum of Fine Arts, Stockholm, Department of Drawings and Prints, nos. 205 and 207, 1980.

27. Gothenburg Museum of Art, Department of Drawings and Prints, nos. 1 and 2, 1923. These two sketches show an animal mask (polar bear) and the Eskimo chief dancing.

28. The 37 sheets owned by Gösta Nystroem (and later by his oldest daughter) were purchased by the National Museum of Fine Arts in Stockholm for 96,500 Swedish crowns in 1980 (equivalent to about 22,800 U.S. dollars at the time) from a private gallery in Stockholm. They are since then being kept at the Department of Drawings and Prints and were, for the first time, exhibited in their totality together with the two sketches owned by the Gothenburg Museum of Art at the Malmö Konsthall, Sweden, from 26 December 1987 to 7 February 1988. See note 16.

29. See note 19.

30. Björn Springfeldt, preface in the Malmö Konsthall exh. cat., *La Mer glaciale,* 1987. See notes 16 and 28.

31. The first performance of *La Création du monde* took place on 25 October 1923. See Häger, *Rolf de Marés svenska balett,* 41.

32. Ahlstrand, *GAN,* 77, for instance.

33. Ahlstrand, *GAN,* 154: "Jag vill ha rörelse framför allt. Den statiska skönheten är mig främmande. Det måste till varje pris röra sig." ("Above all there must be movement. The static beauty is alien to me. Movement is absolutely necessary for me." Author's translation.)

34. About Lindgren, see notes 14 and 16.

35. GAN's *Folk Songs* is an album of unique beauty that contains handwritten texts and illustrations (illuminations) of old Swedish romantic folk songs, executed by GAN with the patience of a monk in his Paris studio during his last year in Paris. They show with all accuracy GAN's passion and great gift for working out decorative schemes in detail in a style that is a personal mixture between the cubism to which GAN has been so dedicated and to the medieval, primarily Gothic art that he had studied with intense interest at the Musée du Louvre and in other Paris museums, including the Bibliothèque Nationale. The *Folk Songs* are a splendid culmination of the five years that GAN spent in Paris, a true landmark in his artistic career that partly evolved out of his sketches for *La Mer glaciale.*

Ballets Suédois Productions

CHRONOLOGY

Compiled by Nancy Van Norman Baer and Tirza True Latimer

The premiere performances of all Ballets Suédois productions were presented in Paris at the Théâtre des Champs-Elysées. The first season was preceded by a solo concert performed by company choreographer Jean Börlin at the Comédie des Champs-Elysées (a secondary auditorium in the theater) on 25 March 1920. The program consisted of the following dance pieces: *Arlequin* (Harlequin) to music by Frédéric Chopin, *Danse céleste* (Celestial Dance) to Léo Delibes's *Lakmé, Sculpture négre* (African Sculpture) to a "Poem-Nocturn" by Alexander Scriabin, *Danse suédoise* (Swedish Dance) to Swedish folk melodies, *Danse tzigane* (Gypsy Dance) to Camille Saint-Saens' *Henri VIII Ballet, Devant la mort* (Before Death) to *Saint Francis of Assisi Walking on Water* by Franz Liszt, and *Derviche* (Dervish) to *La danse de Salomé* by Alexander Glazunov. Orchestral interludes featuring the music of Claude Debussy, Alexander Borodin, Maurice Ravel, Wilhelm Peterson Berger, Florent Schmitt, and Désiré-Emile Inghelbrecht were performed between dances.

● **1920**

JEUX
(Games)
Choreography: Jean Börlin
Music: Claude Debussy
Libretto: Originally developed in 1913 by Léon Bakst and Vaslav Nijinsky for Serge Diaghilev's Ballets Russes
Costumes: Jeanne Lanvin
Decor: Pierre Bonnard
Premiere: 25 October 1920

DERVICHES
(Dervishes)
Choreography: Jean Börlin
Music: Alexander Glazunov
Costumes: Jean Börlin, executed by Germaine Bonafous
Decor: Georges Mouveau after Persian miniatures
Premiere: 25 October 1920

IBERIA
Choreography: Jean Börlin
Music: Isaac Albeniz, orchestrated by Désiré-Emile Inghelbrecht
Costumes: Théophile Alexandre Steinlen, executed by Germaine Bonafous
Decor: Théophile Alexandre Steinlen
Premiere: 25 October 1920

NUIT DE SAINT JEAN
(Saint John's Night, or Midsummer Night's Revel)
Choreography: Jean Börlin
Music: Hugo Alfvén
Libretto: Jean Börlin
Costumes: Nils Dardel, executed by Germaine Bonafous
Curtain and decor: Nils Dardel
Premiere: 25 October 1920

MAISON DE FOUS
(Madhouse)
Choreography: Jean Börlin
Music: Viking Dahl
Libretto: Jean Börlin
Costumes and decor: Nils Dardel
Premiere: 8 November 1920

LE TOMBEAU DE COUPERIN
(The Tomb of Couperin)
Choreography: Jean Börlin, based on eighteenth-century court dances
Music: Maurice Ravel
Costumes and decor: Pierre Laprade
Premiere: 8 November 1920
Note: Ravel composed this score as a memorial to the French composer François Couperin (1668-1733).

Nuit de Saint Jean, Paris, 1920, cat. no. 188.

EL GRECO
Choreography: Jean Börlin
Music: Désiré-Emile Inghelbrecht
Libretto: Jean Börlin
Costumes: Jean Börlin and Nils Dardel after Domenikos Theotocopoulos (known as El Greco), executed by Germaine Bonafous
Decor: Georges Mouveau, after a painting by El Greco, *View of Toledo* (ca. 1610)
Premiere: 18 November 1920

PAS DE DEUX
Choreography: Jean Börlin, inspired by Michel Fokine
Music: Chopin, orchestrated by Eugène Bigot
Premiere: 18 November 1920
Note: In 1921 this classical ensemble work was presented in an expanded version entitled *Chopin.*

LES VIERGES FOLLES
(The Foolish Virgins)
Choreography: Jean Börlin
Music: Kurt Atterberg, based on Swedish folk melodies
Libretto: Kurt Atterberg and Einar Nerman, based on a biblical parable (Matthew 25)
Costumes and decor: Einar Nerman, after eighteenth- and nineteenth-century Dalecarlian murals (a style of folk painting) conserved in the Nordic Museum, Stockholm.
Premiere: 18 November 1920

● **1921**

LA BOÎTE À JOUJOUX
(The Toy-Box)
Choreography: Jean Börlin
Music: Claude Debussy, orchestrated by André Caplet
Libretto: André Hellé
Costumes and decor: André Hellé
Premiere: 15 February 1921

Note: This ballet was first designed and produced by André Hellé on 10 December 1919 at the Théâtre Lyrique du Vaudeville, Paris.

L'HOMME ET SON DÉSIR
(Man and His Desire)
Choreography: Jean Börlin
Music: Darius Milhaud
Libretto: Paul Claudel
Costumes: Audrey [Andrée] Parr, executed by Marie Muelle
Decor: Audrey [Andrée] Parr, executed by Georges Mouveau
Premiere: 6 June 1921

LES MARIÉS DE LA TOUR EIFFEL
(The Newlyweds on the Eiffel Tower)
Choreography: Jean Börlin
Music: Georges Auric, Arthur Honegger, Darius Milhaud, Francis Poulenc, Germaine Tailleferre
Libretto: Jean Cocteau
Costumes: Jean Hugo, assisted by Valentine Gross Hugo; executed by Jean Hugo (painted masks), Bertbelin, and Max Weldy
Decor: Irène Lagut, executed by Georges Mouveau
Narration: Marcel Herrand and Pierre Bertin
Premiere: 18 June 1921

DANSGILLE
(Dance Feast, or Dances at a Gathering)
Choreography: Jean Börlin
Music: Eugène Bigot, after Swedish folk melodies
Costumes: native Swedish designs
Decor: an enlargement of a Swedish folk painting entitled *Dansgille* (1848) by Olof Andersson. The painting was selected by Börlin from the collection of the Nordic Museum, Stockholm.
Premiere: 20 November 1921

CHOPIN
Choreography: Jean Börlin, inspired by Michel Fokine
Music: Chopin, orchestrated by Eugène Bigot
Premiere: 20 November 1921
Note: See 1920, *Pas de deux*

● 1922

SKATING RINK
Choreography: Jean Börlin
Music: Arthur Honegger
Libretto: after a futurist poem by Ricciotto Canudo published in *Mercure de France*, 15 May 1920, as "Skating Ring at Tabarin/ballet-on-skates"
Curtain, costumes, and decor: Fernand Léger
Premiere: 20 January 1922

● 1923

MARCHAND D'OISEAUX
(The Bird Seller)
Choreography: Jean Börlin
Music: Germaine Tailleferre
Libretto: Hélène Perdriat
Costumes and decor: Hélène Perdriat
Premiere: 25 May 1923

OFFERLUNDEN
(The Sacrificial Grove)
Choreography: Jean Börlin
Music: Algot Haquinius
Libretto: Jean Börlin
Costumes and decor: Gunnar Hallström
Premiere: 25 May 1923

LA CRÉATION DU MONDE
(The Creation of the World)
Choreography: Jean Börlin, inspired by Rolf de Maré's documentary films of African dances
Music: Darius Milhaud
Libretto: Blaise Cendrars, based on a composite of several Fang origin myths from his 1921 collection *Anthologie nègre* (African Anthology).
Curtain: Fernand Léger
Costumes: Fernand Léger, executed by Marie Muelle
Decor: Fernand Léger, executed by Marcel Guérin
Premiere: 25 October 1923

WITHIN THE QUOTA
Choreography: Jean Börlin
Music: Cole Porter, orchestrated by Charles Koechlin
Libretto: Gerald Murphy
Costumes and decor: Gerald Murphy, assisted by Sara Wiborg Murphy
Premiere: 25 October 1923

● 1924

LE ROSEAU
(The Reed Player)
Choreography: Jean Börlin
Music: Daniel Lazarus
Libretto: after a legend recounted by thirteenth-century Persian mystic and poet Jalal ud-Din Rumi in Book 1 of *Mathnawi*
Costumes: Alexander Alexeieff, executed by Marie Vasilieff
Decor: Alexander Alexeieff after Persian miniatures, executed by Numa and Chazot
Premiere: 19 November 1924

LE PORCHER
(The Swineherd)
Choreography: Jean Börlin
Music: Swedish folk melodies, orchestrated by Pierre-Octave Ferroud
Libretto: after a fairy tale, "The Swineherd," by Hans Christian Andersen
Costumes: Alexander Alexeieff, executed by Marie Vasilieff
Decor: Alexander Alexeieff, executed by Numa and Chazot
Premiere: 19 November 1924

LE TOURNOI SINGULIER
(The Singular Tournament)
Choreography: Jean Börlin
Music: Roland-Manuel [Roland Alexis Manuel Lévy]
Libretto: Roland-Manuel, after a sixteenth-century prose poem by Louise Labé entitled "Le Débat de folie et d'amour" (The Debate between Madness and Love)
Costumes: Tsuguharu-Léonard Foujita, executed by Marie Vasilieff
Decor: Tsuguharu-Léonard Foujita, executed by Numa and Chazot
Premiere: 19 November 1924

LA JARRE
(The Jar)
Choreography: Jean Börlin
Music: Alfredo Casella
Libretto: Jean Börlin, after the short story "La Giarra" by Luigi Pirandello
Costumes: Giorgio de Chirico, executed by Marie Vasilieff
Decor: Giorgio de Chirico, executed by Numa and Chazot
Premiere: 19 November 1924

RELÂCHE
(Cancelled)
Choreography: Jean Börlin
Music: Erik Satie
Libretto: Francis Picabia
Curtain: Francis Picabia
Costumes: Francis Picabia, with the exception of Edith Bonsdorff's gown, by Jacques Doucet
Decor: Francis Picabia; light panel executed by the firm Paz & Silva
Cinematography: René Clair (see *Entr'acte* below)
Premiere: 4 December 1924
Note: Word plays and puns are the essence of dada satire. The multiple senses of the word *relâche* (cancelled, relaxation, break, letting go) all reverberate in Picabia's title. *Relâche* also often means "no performance," as when a house is dark for the days immediately preceding a new attraction.

ENTR'ACTE
(Intermission)
Direction and editing: René Clair
Camera: Jimmy Berliet
Assistant: Georges Lacombe
Music: Erik Satie
Script: René Clair, based on a scenario by Francis Picabia
Producer: Rolf de Maré
Cast: Marcel Achard, Jean Börlin, Georges Charensol, Marcel Duchamp, Inger Friis, Roger Lebon, Mamy, Rolf de Maré, Francis Picabia, Erik Satie, Pierre Scize, Louis Touchagues, Man Ray, miscellaneous passers-by and acquaintances
Premiere: 4 December 1924
Note: This twenty-one-minute film was shown in place of an intermission during the performance of *Relâche*. The ballet's one-minute cinematic prologue, *Projectionette*, has been erroneously spliced on to the beginning of *Entr'acte*, following the credits. Clair conceived the prologue as an autonomous work, however.

Ballets Suédois

DANCERS IN THE COMPANY

The following list of dancers who performed with the Ballets Suédois from 1920 to 1925 is reprinted from Rolf de Maré, *Les Ballets Suédois dans l'art contemporain* (Paris: Editions du Trianon, 1931). The names of other dancers who performed with the company, according to ballet programs, are given parenthetically. The list is presumably incomplete since programs specify only dancers in principal roles and do not name all members of the corps de ballet.

Female Dancers

(Allan), Carina Ari, Siva Blomkvist, Edith Bonsdorff, Irma Calson, Helga Dahl, Jolanda Figoni, Dagmar Forslin, Inger Friis, Jenny Hasselquist, Margareta Johansson, Greta Kähr, Ingeborg Kähr, Klara Kjellblad, Berta Krantz, Valborg Larson, Astrid Lindgren, Greta Lundberg, Signe Malmberg, Therese Petterson, Elsie Schwarck, Signe Selid, Torborg Stjerner, Ebon Strandin, Margit Wåhlander, Anna Wikström.

Male Dancers

Ture Andersson, Sam Blomkvist, Jean Börlin, John Carlberg, Kristian Dahl, Rupert Doone, Paul Eltorp, Kaarlo Eronen, Robert Ford, (Bob Giller), Walther Junk, Holger Mehnen, Toivo Niskanen, Nils Östman, Kaj Smith, Léon Stetler, (Tor Stettler), (Eric Viber), Axel Witzansky, Paul Witzansky.

Jean Börlin in the Royal Opera Ballet, Stockholm, production of *Le Dieu bleu*, 1919, cat. no. 175.

Ballets Suédois

ITINERARY

During its five-year existence, the Ballets Suédois presented a total of 2,766 performances in 157 cities in Europe and the United States. At least thirty-two visual artists, sixteen writers, twenty-three musicians, and forty-five dancers contributed to the creation of the company's twenty-three productions. The translated and annotated itinerary below first appeared in *Les Ballets Suédois dans l'art contemporain.*

• 1920
France: Paris
United Kingdom: London

• 1921
France: Paris
Spain: Barcelona, Valencia, Madrid, Valladolid, Bilboa, Santander, Corunna, El Ferrol, Orense, Vigo, Pontevedra, Santiago
Belgium: Brussels
France: Paris, Roubaix, Douai, Valenciennes, Lille, Orléans, Nantes, Le Mans, Rochefort, Limoges, Périgueux, Bordeaux, Pau, Tarbes, Carcassonne, Sète, Nimes, Montpellier, Narbonne, Toulouse, Perpignan, Béziers, Avignon, Nice, Nimes (return engagement), Saint-Etienne, Dijon, Troyes, Nancy

• 1922
France: Paris
Germany: Berlin
Austria: Vienna
Hungary: Budapest
Germany: Berlin, Cologne, Düsseldorf, Hamburg
Sweden: Stockholm
France: Besançon, Montreux
Switzerland: Geneva, Lausanne
France: Evian, Aix-les-Bains, Dijon, Le Havre, Trouville, Cabourg, Caen, Cherbourg, Paramé, Rennes, Saint-Nazaire, La Rochelle, Fouras, Royan, Arcachon, Biarritz, Angoulême
Sweden: Malmö, Helsingborg, Gothenburg
Denmark: Copenhagen
Norway: Oslo
United Kingdom: London, Brighton, Hull, Newcastle, Glasgow

• 1923
France: Etampes
Italy: Milan, Brescia, Genoa, Florence, Forli, Ravenna, Pesaro, Bologna, Verona, Udine, Trieste, Gorizia, Venice, Treviso, Vicenza, Mantua, Modena, Piacenza, Turin
France: Paris
United States: New York, Philadelphia, Washington, New York (return engagement)

• 1924
United States: Pennsylvania: Easton, Reading, Allentown, Scranton, Harrisburg, York, Lebanon, Williamsport, Wilkes-Barre; New York: Albany, Geneva, Oswego, Syracuse, Rochester, Utica, Batavia; Ohio: Elyria, Toledo, Lima, Dayton, Columbus, Coshocton; Pennsylvania: New Philadelphia, Newcastle, Cumberland, Altoona, Allentown (return engagement)
France: Paris

• 1925
France: Paris
Belgium: Brussels, Namur
France: Brest, Lorient, Rennes, Le Mans, Nantes, Angers, Nantes (return engagement), Saint-Nazaire, La Rochelle, Angoulême, Limoges, Brive, Arcachon, Bordeaux, Bayonne, Pau, Toulouse, Nice, Menton, Grasse, Cannes, Saint-Raphaël, Toulon, Hyères, Salon, Marseilles, Avignon, Lyons, Dijon, Troyes, Epinal, Verdun, Epernay

Ballets Suédois

PLOT SUMMARIES

Compiled by Tirza True Latimer

The ballets are listed in the order in which they were originally presented, according to *Les Ballets Suédois dans l'art contemporain* and various souvenir programs. Plot summaries have been drawn from these fundamental documents. Quoted passages are translations of descriptions found in the same sources. The performances all premiered at the Thèâtre des Champs-Elysées, Paris. For additional details, refer to the Chronology.

JEUX (Games), first performed 25 October 1920

A young tennis player searching for a lost ball is waylaid by two attractive young women. After a dalliance in the park the athlete returns to his tennis.

DERVICHES (Dervishes), first performed 25 October 1920

In a golden mosque dervishes pray. They bend and unbend "slowly like stems of very heavy flowers." And then, upright and swirling, the dancers "are carried away by the music," ultimately "throwing themselves face down against the earth."

IBERIA, first performed 25 October 1920

Dances evoking Spain are performed in three Iberian settings: the "seaport with an architecture of gigantic ships," the bucolic surroundings of a wayside tavern, and the city plaza in the shadow of Seville's majestic cathedral.

NUIT DE SAINT JOHN (Saint John's Night, or Midsummer's Night Revel), first performed 25 October 1920

Villagers dance around a flowering maypole, pausing occasionally to toast each other with strong drink. During "a night which lasts only a few instants" on this longest day of the year, they drift off to sleep. With the first light of dawn the celebration recommences.

MAISON DE FOUS (Madhouse), first performed 8 November 1920

A young woman wanders into an insane asylum. She encounters inmates suffering from various forms of madness, "the follies that are in all human beings." She falls in love with a deranged young prince, who ends up strangling her.

TOMBEAU DE COUPERIN (The Tomb of Couperin), first performed 8 November 1920

In a formal garden setting dancers dressed in eighteenth-century costumes perform a sequence of formal steps derived from the minuet and other court dances.

EL GRECO, first performed 18 November 1920

"A spectacle of synthesis in which painting, action, and music intermingle harmoniously in a complete art through a series of mimed scenes. . . ." The dancers present a collection of *tableaux vivants* interpreting several of the Spanish master's dolorous images, including *The Burial of the Count of Orgaz* (1586).

PAS DE DEUX, first performed 18 November 1920

A suite of classical dances performed to a medley of Chopin's compositions. *Note:* see *Chopin.*

LES VIERGES FOLLES (The Foolish Virgins), first performed 18 November 1920

The wise and the foolish virgins of the biblical parable are recast in Swedish folk guise. A maiden, accompanied by the virgins, sets out in the night to meet her betrothed. The foolish virgins, cavorting, leave the flames of their lamps unprotected and burn all their oil, while the wise virgins guard their flames and conserve their resources. The foolish virgins vainly beg the wise virgins for oil; denied, they resort to searching elsewhere. In the meantime the betrothed arrives to find his beloved illuminated by the wise virgins. The wise virgins escort the couple into a chapel to be wed. When the foolish virgins return they are not permitted to join the wedding party.

LA BOÎTE À JOUJOUX (The Toy-Box), first performed 15 February 1921

In a toy shop at night, harlequins, lead soldiers, mechanical toys, and puppets wake up and dance to the music. A romantic drama unfolds: A soldier and Pulcinello compete for the hand of Columbine. She chooses the soldier. They marry and prosper as sheep farmers. The rejected suitor becomes a gamekeeper.
Note: The word *boite* (box) is also slang for "night club." The title thus has a double sense: "toy-box" and "toys' night club".

L'HOMME ET SON DÉSIR (Man and His Desire), first performed 6 June 1921

In the words of the author, Paul Claudel, "There is nothing new in the subject of the drama, not any more than in the most audacious tragedies. It is the theme of a man trapped in a passion. . . , in a desire, . . .who attempts vainly to escape as if from a prison with invisible bars." Sleeping and awake, he is tormented by women representing Memory, Imagination, Illusion, Desire, and Exile. He is finally released "when a woman who is at once the image of Death and of Love comes to take him with her."

LES MARIÉS DE LA TOUR EIFFEL (The Newlyweds on the Eiffel Tower), first performed 18 June 1921

A wedding party poses for photos on the platform of the Eiffel Tower. Each time a voice calls "watch the birdie," an interloper pops out of the hunch-backed photographer's giant camera. Chaos ensues. The uninvited guests include an ostrich, a hunter, a fat boy, a lion, human telegrams, and a bathing beauty. The fat boy (Child of the Future), angrily pelts the adults. The lion eats a wedding guest (the General). Two "phonographic pavilions" issuing comments in "mechanical voices manifesting their entirely artificial intelligence" flank the absurd scene. One by one the bizarre gate-crashers retreat into the camera.

DANSGILLE (Dance Feast, or Dances at a Gathering), first performed 20 November 1921

A "peasantry multicolored, fresh, and healthy" in native Swedish dress performs folk dances to traditional tunes. The backdrop, realized in the style of a nineteenth-century Dalecarlian painting (a style of folk painting), contributes to the Nordic flavor of the festivities.

CHOPIN, first performed 20 November 1921

An ensemble work modeled on *Les Sylphides,* a classical production conceived for Diaghilev's Ballets Russes by Michel Fokine in 1909.
Note: Chopin was an expanded version of *Pas de deux.*

SKATING RINK, first performed 20 January 1922

"The whirlwind of skaters is an allegory for the more desperate whirlwind of life. . . . Groups of skaters weave in and out of each other when suddenly a man stands out: the Poet, the Madman. A woman is attracted by the energy he radiates. The woman's lover tries vainly to win her back, but [she and the Madman are] elusive. Little by little, in spite of himself, the lover gives up and is pulled back into the general swirling. . . . The Madman. . . , triumphant, carries the woman away . . . within the indifference of the crowd which continues to spin."

MARCHAND D'OISEAUX (The Bird Seller), first performed 25 May 1923

Two sisters, one haughty and one humble, find bouquets from mysterious suitors on their doorstep. Each chooses the bouquet to her taste: the haughty sister the expensive roses and the humble sister the simple wildflowers. The suitor who left the wildflowers, a young bird seller, introduces himself. The haughty sister shuns him, but the humble sister takes his arm. The suitor who left the roses, a rich stranger, then appears. A schoolgirl tears off his mask, revealing the face of a fat old shopkeeper from town. The humble sister and her handsome bird seller drift blissfully offstage, arm in arm, leaving the disappointed haughty sister behind.

OFFERLUNDEN (The Sacrificial Grove), first performed 25 May 1923

"This ballet . . . evokes scenes from the lives of Bronze Age Vikings. In a prehistoric forest, the sacred flame has gone out. . . . The rites, dances [and] supplications [of the Vikings] are futile. Ultimately, the self-sacrificial death of their chieftain rekindles the flame."

LA CRÉATION DU MONDE (The Creation of the World), first performed 25 October 1923

Three giant deities circle around a formless mass. The incantations of these gods — Nzamé, Mébère, and Nkwa — cause the mass to separate and evolve into living creatures; an elephant, an ape, a leopard, a tortoise, a beetle, a bird, a crab, and some monkeys take shape. A woman and a man rise up and embrace. "The couple," according to author Blaise Cendrars, "isolates itself in a kiss that carries them like a wave. Then it is spring."

WITHIN THE QUOTA, first performed 25 October 1923

A Swedish immigrant steps off the boat in New York and encounters a parade of characters representing his new country's most stereotypical citizens, including "an American Heiress, a Gentleman of Color, a Jazzbaby, a Cowboy." Order is maintained by a character assuming various guises: "Social Reformer, Revenue-Agent, . . . or Sheriff." The foreigner meets America's Sweetheart (a Mary Pickford look-alike), and they elope.

LE ROSEAU (The Reed Player), first performed 19 November 1924

According to a Persian fable, Khedad, listening to a flute player's music, imagines that the "earthly love" of Suleika will soothe his troubled heart. A different melody convinces him that his longing is of a spiritual nature. He separates from Suleika to follow, through prayer, a path of "eternal nostalgia."

LE PORCHER (The Swineherd), first performed 19 November 1924

The prince of a minor kingdom wishes to marry a great king's daughter. He offers her exotic gifts but she is unimpressed. He then woos her disguised as a swineherd and wins her affection. The king is outraged and chases his daughter and the swineherd away. The prince reveals his true identity to the princess only to abandon her in revenge for her initial indifference.

LE TOURNOI SINGULIER (The Singular Tournament), first performed 19 November 1924

A modern golf course serves as a setting for the classical myth of Love blinded by Folly. Folly takes a wild swing and hits Eros in the eye with her golf ball. Eros goes blind. His mother, Venus, obliges Folly to lead Eros around by the hand forever after.

LA JARRE (The Jar), first performed 19 November 1924

Don Lollo, a rich landholder, orders Zi Dima, the hunchbacked handyman, to fix his broken olive-oil jar. Zi Dima climbs inside the ample vessel to mend it from within. When Zi Dima's hunch gets caught on the lip of the jar, trapping him inside, Don Lollo refuses to consider breaking the pot to release him. Zi Dima keeps his spirits up by singing with a group of sympathetic bystanders that has gathered around the jar. The singing gets louder and louder as the night goes on. Don Lollo, his sleep disturbed by the racket in his courtyard, storms out to silence the assembly. In the dark he accidentally kicks the jar, which breaks, freeing Zi Dima.

RELÂCHE (Cancelled), first performed 4 December 1924, with ENTR'ACTE (Intermission)

Relâche consists of a filmed prologue, two ballet acts separated by a cinematic intermission *(Entr'acte)*, and a finale described enigmatically as the *Queue-de-chien* (Dog's Tail). In the one-minute prologue a cannon is shot at the audience by two angels (Picabia and Satie). The curtain rises to reveal a towering panel of lights, which flash intermittently and blind the audience. In the course of this antiballet's nonnarrative scenario, a man (Man Ray) gets up from his chair now and then to measure the stage. A pacing fireman puffs on a cigarette. (*pompier*, fireman, is a French figure of speech meaning "conventional academic artist.") A flashy woman (Edith Bonsdorff) in a sequined evening gown (by Jacques Doucet) gets up from a seat in the auditorium and dances a few steps without music. When the music begins she stops dancing. She sits down on the stage to smoke. A paralyzed man (Jean Börlin) is cured by the sight of her. Gents in evening dress stroll onstage from the audience. They form a human bridge, and the flashy woman climbs over their backs. They carry her offstage.

The cinematic interval, *Entr'acte* by René Clair, consists of a series of absurd vignettes that follow each other in rapid succession. Two men filmed from above (Marcel Duchamp and Man Ray) play chess. A juggler juggles. A boxer's gloved fists jab at the camera. The pirouettes of a bearded ballerina (Picabia) are observed through a glass peephole in the floor. A hunter (Jean Börlin) shoots an ostrich egg held up by a jet of water. A pigeon flies out of the broken egg and makes itself at home on the hunter's feathered cap. A second hunter (Picabia) takes aim at the pigeon, fires, misses, and shoots the first hunter in the head. A funeral procession forms. Mourners cracking morbid jokes accompany a camel-drawn hearse decorated with hams and wreaths of bread. The hearse breaks loose and careens across a tumbling landscape with the mourners in pursuit. The coffin slides off the hearse and bursts open. A magician (Jean Börlin) steps out, all smiles. He waves his wand and everyone disappears, including himself. The screen goes blank and then announces "Fin." But of course it is not the end; the magician bursts headlong through the screen. The manager (Rolf de Maré) pushes him back through the hole in the screen, restoring order so that *Relâche* may continue.

The curtain falls. It is scrawled with provocative slogans like "Do you prefer the ballet at the Opera?"and "Poor imbeciles." The curtain rises and act 2 begins. The "dancers who dare not dance" continue not to dance. The flashy woman is carried back onstage by the gents, accompanied by a nurse. The fireman, still smoking, pours water back and forth from one bucket to another. The gents take off their clothes, exposing polka-dotted long johns. The flashy woman gathers the clothes in a wheelbarrow. She and one of the men crown a member of the audience with a wreath of orange blossoms. A statuette placed among the gents acts as a surrogate for the flashy woman. Picabia, for his curtain call, drives Satie around the stage in a miniature Citroën. As for the famous Dog's Tail, "no one ever saw hide nor hair of it," or so said René Clair *(L'Avant-Scène du cinéma* 86, November 1968, 18).

Checklist of the Exhibition

Works on paper or canvas are arranged alphabetically by artist. Production titles are given in their original form. The titles of the principal roles, as listed in ballet programs, are capitalized. Descriptions of roles not specifically listed are not capitalized. Unless otherwise mentioned all works are from the collection of the Dansmuseet, Stockholm.

1
Anonymous
Program cover design for the Ballets Suédois: Jean Börlin in his leading roles, 1923
Watercolor, gouache, and photo-collage on paper, 26.5 x 20 cm

2
Anonymous
Jean Börlin in *Dansgille*, *Derviches*, *Jeux*, and *Iberia*, 1921
Four oil-on-canvas cutouts affixed to metal, each ca. 34 x 16.5 cm

ALEXANDER ALEXEIEFF
(Kazan, Russia 1901–1982 Paris, France)

3
Costume design for the Emperor in *Le Porcher*, 1924
Graphite and india ink on paper, 35 x 24 cm

4
Costume design for the Prince in *Le Porcher*, 1924
Graphite and india ink on paper, 35.5 x 24 cm

5 *(illus. page 30)*
Costume design for a male dancer (Khedad) in *Le Roseau*, 1924
Graphite, watercolor, gouache, and india ink on paper, 47.5 x 31.5 cm

6 *(illus. page 30)*
Costume design for the Old Musician in *Le Roseau*, 1924
Graphite, watercolor, gouache and india ink on paper, 47.5 x 31.5 cm

7
Costume design for a Slave in *Le Roseau*, 1924
Graphite, watercolor, gouache, and india ink on paper , 47 x 31.5 cm

8
Costume design for a female dancer (Suleika) in *Le Roseau*, 1924
Graphite, watercolor, gouache, and india ink on paper, 47.5 x 31.5 cm

GIORGIO DE CHIRICO
(Volos, Greece 1888–1978 Rome, Italy

9 *(illus. page 34)*
Set design for *La Jarre*, 1924
Tempera on canvas, 25.5 x 34 cm

10
Costume design for the Daughter of the Patron in *La Jarre*, 1924
Graphite and gouache on cardboard, 34 x 26 cm

11 *(illus. page 32)*
Two costume designs for Young Lads in *La Jarre*, 1924
Gouache on cardboard, each 34 x 26 cm

12
Costume design for the Hunchback in *La Jarre*, 1924
Gouache on cardboard, 34 x 26 cm

13
Two costume designs for Peasants in *La Jarre*, 1924
Graphite and gouache on cardboard, each 34 x 26 cm

14
Design for a stage prop for *La Jarre*, 1924
Gouache on wood panel, 34 x 26 cm

PAUL COLIN
(Nancy, France 1892–1985 Nogent-sur-Marne, France)

15 *(illus. page 67)*
Poster: Jean Börlin, 1924
Color lithograph, 35 x 27 cm

16
Poster: Jean Börlin, 1925
Color lithograph, 120 x 80 cm

MIGUEL COVARRUBIAS
(Mexico City 1904–1957 Mexico City)

17 *(illus. page 115)*
Caricature of Jean Börlin in *Within the Quota*, 1923
Graphite, watercolor, gouache, and india ink on paper, 35.5 x 23.5 cm

NILS [VON] DARDEL
(Stockholm, Sweden 1888–1943 New York, USA)

18 *(illus. page 41)*
Portrait of Rolf de Maré, 1916
Oil on cardboard, 61 x 50 cm

19
Jean Börlin in the solo dance *Arlequin*, 1919
Graphite, watercolor, and gouache on paper, 50 x 38 cm

20 *(illus. page 59)*
Set design for *Nuit de Saint Jean*, 1920
Graphite, watercolor, and gouache on paper, 50 x 65 cm

21
Set design for *Nuit de Saint Jean*, 1920
Graphite, watercolor, and gouache on paper, 52 x 68 cm

22
Costume design for a young girl in *Nuit de Saint Jean*, 1920
Graphite, watercolor, and gouache on paper, 25 x 13 cm

23 *(illus. page 18)*
Backdrop design for *Maison de fous*, 1920
Graphite, watercolor, and gouache on paper, 43 x 60 cm

24 *(illus. page 57)*
Curtain design for *Nuit de Saint Jean* and *Dansgille*, 1921
Graphite, watercolor, and gouache on paper, 57.5 x 46 cm

25 *(illus. page 45)*
The Executioner or the Triumph of the Ballets Suédois, 1920
Graphite, watercolor, and gouache on paper, 31 x 34.5 cm

H. DAVEN
(French)

26
L'idée du Ballet de Börlin réalisée par Picabia (The Idea for a Ballet by Börlin realized by Picabia), 1924
Jean Börlin trouvant une ideé de Ballet, (Jean Börlin finds the idea for a Ballet), 1924
India ink on paper, each 21 x 13.7 cm

ELDSTEN [NÉE FEUERSTEIN]

27 *(illus. page 168)*
Design for poster: *Ballets Suédois*, ca. 1921
Watercolor, gouache, and india ink on paper, 31.5 x 48 cm

TSUGUHARU-LÉONARD FOUJITA
(Tokyo, Japan 1886–1968 Zurich, Switzerland)

28 *(illus. page 35)*
Set design for *Le Tournoi singulier*, 1924
Graphite on paper , 17 x 24 cm

29 *(illus. page 82)*
Costume design for Folly in *Le Tournoi singulier*, 1924
Graphite, watercolor, and india ink on paper, 25 x 16 cm

30
Costume design for a Caddy in *Le Tournoi singulier*, 1924
Graphite, watercolor, and india ink on paper, 23 x 12 cm

31
Portrait of the composer Roland-Manuel [Roland Alexis Manuel Lévy], 1924
India ink on paper, 18.5 x 12.5 cm

32
Self-portrait, 1924
India ink on paper, 19 x 13 cm

SERGE GLADKY
(Russian)

33
Poster design for Jean Börlin in *Cercle Eternel*, 1929
Crayon and pastel on paper, 60 x 49 cm

34
Poster: Jean Börlin in *Cercle Eternel*, 1929
Color lithograph , 83 x 60 cm

GUNNAR HALLSTRÖM
(Stockholm, Sweden 1875–1943 Stockholm, Sweden)

35 *(illus. page 64)*
Three costume designs for women in *Offerlunden*, 1923
Graphite, watercolor, and india ink wash on paper, 35.7 x 25.5, 29 x 24.5, and 35 x 25 cm

36
Costume design for a woman with a drinking cup in *Offerlunden*, 1923
Graphite, watercolor, and gouache on paper, 48 x 30 cm

37 *(illus. page 65)*
Costume design for two figures in white in *Offerlunden*, 1923
Graphite and watercolor on paper, 45.5 x 27 cm

38
Costume design for a female figure with a sword in *Offerlunden*, 1923
Graphite, watercolor, india ink, ink wash, and metallic paint on paper, 36 x 25.5 cm

39
Costume detail from *Offerlunden*, Headdress, 1923
Graphite, watercolor, gouache, and metallic paint on paper, 36 x 25.5 cm

40
Costume detail from *Offerlunden*, Drinking vessel, 1923
Graphite and watercolor on paper, 36 x 25.5 cm

ANDRÉ HELLÉ
(Paris, France 1871–1945)

41
Set design for *La Boîte à joujoux*, 1921
Graphite, watercolor, and gouache on paper, 40 x 54 cm

42
Costume design for Harlequin in *La Boîte à joujoux*, 1921
Graphite, watercolor, and india ink on paper, 26.5 x 20 cm

43
Costume design for Pulcinella in *La Boîte à joujoux*, 1921
Graphite, watercolor, and india ink on paper, 26 x 20 cm

44
Costume design for the Tiger in *La Boîte à joujoux*, 1921
Graphite, watercolor, and india ink on paper, 23 x 29 cm

JEAN HUGO
(Paris, France 1894–1984 Lunel, France)

45 *(illus. page 25)*
Costume design for the Ostrich in *Les Mariés de la Tour Eiffel*, 1921
Watercolor, gouache, india ink, and collage on tracing paper and paper affixed to linen, 29.5 x 21.5 cm

46 *(illus. page 25)*
Costume design for the Lion in *Les Mariés de la Tour Eiffel*, 1921
Graphite, ink, watercolor, and gouache on tracing paper and paper affixed to linen, 28 x 21 cm

47
Costume design for the Bride in *Les Mariés de la Tour Eiffel*, 1921
Graphite and gouache on paper affixed to linen, 28.5 x 21.5 cm

48
Costume design for the Bridegroom in *Les Mariés de la Tour Eiffel*, 1921
Graphite, gouache, and india ink on paper affixed to linen, 29 x 22 cm

49 *(illus. page 11)*
Costume design for a female dancer in blue in *Les Mariés de la Tour Eiffel*, 1921
Graphite and gouache on paper, 30 x 21.2 cm

50
Costume design for the Bathing Girl from Trouville in *Les Mariés de la Tour Eiffel*, 1923
Graphite, gouache, and india ink on paper, 29 x 22 cm

51
Costume design for the General in *Les Mariés de la Tour Eiffel*, 1923
Graphite, gouache, and india ink on paper, 29 x 22 cm

52
Costume design for the Huntsman in *Les Mariés de la Tour Eiffel*, 1923
Graphite, watercolor, and gouache on paper, 29 x 22 cm

PER KROHG
(Asgardstrand, Norway 1889–1965 Oslo, Norway)

53
Poster: *Jean Börlin/24 October 1920*
Color lithograph, imp. Publicité Wall, Paris, 153 x 114 cm

IRÈNE LAGUT
(Born Paris, France 1893–?)

54 *(illus. page 23)*
Set design for *Les Mariés de la Tour Eiffel*, 1921
Graphite, gouache, and india ink on cardboard, 32.5 x 36.5 cm

PIERRE LAPRADE [PIERRE COFFINHAL-LAPRADE]
(Narbonne, France 1875–1931 Fontenay-aux-Roses, France)

55
Set design for *Le Tombeau de Couperin*, 1920
Watercolor and india ink on paper, 14 x 14 cm

56
Two costume designs for women in *Le Tombeau de Couperin*, 1920
Graphite, watercolor, and india ink on paper, each 19.5 x 11.5 cm

FERNAND LÉGER
(Argentan, France 1881–1955 Gif-sur-Yvett, France)

57
Program design, 1923
Graphite, watercolor, gouache, and india ink on paper, 32.5 x 24.5 cm

58
Sketch for program design (figure from *Skating Rink*), 1921
Graphite, watercolor, and ink wash on paper, 10 x 3.3 cm

59 *(illus. page 97)*
Curtain design for *Skating Rink*, 1921
Graphite, watercolor, gouache, and india ink on paper, 40.5 x 48 cm

60 *(illus. page 96)*
Backdrop design for *Skating Rink*, 1921
Graphite, watercolor, gouache, and india ink on paper, 29 x 59 cm

61 *(illus. page 26)*
Set design for *Skating Rink*, 1921
Graphite and watercolor on paper, 22 x 30 cm

62
Costume design for a woman with red hat in *Skating Rink*, 1921
Graphite, watercolor, and india ink on paper, 25 x 16 cm

63 *(illus. page 92)*
Costume design for a woman with green hat in *Skating Rink*, 1921
Graphite, watercolor, gouache, and india ink on paper, 25 x 15.5 cm

64
Costume design for a man in yellow, brown, and blue in *Skating Rink*, 1921
Graphite, watercolor, gouache, and india ink on paper, 22.5 x 14.8 cm

65
Costume design for a man in red, blue, and brown in *Skating Rink*, 1921
Graphite, gouache, and india ink on paper, 22.5 x 14 cm

66
Costume design for a woman in blue and brown in *Skating Rink*, 1921
Graphite, gouache, india ink, and ink wash on paper, 24 x 16 cm

67
Costume design for a woman in blue, red, and grey in *Skating Rink*, 1921
Graphite, gouache, india ink, and ink wash on paper, 22.5 x 14 cm

68 *(illus. page 90)*
Costume design for a woman in white, blue, and brown in *Skating Rink*, 1921
Graphite, gouache, and india ink on paper, 23 x 15 cm

69 *(illus. page 91)*
Costume design for a man in black top hat in *Skating Rink*, 1921
Graphite, gouache, india ink, and ink wash on paper, 25.5 x 15 cm

70
Costume design for a man in red and green with red top hat in *Skating Rink*, 1921
Graphite and watercolor on paper, 23 x 16 cm

71
Costume design for a man in gray top hat in *Skating Rink*, 1921
Graphite, gouache, and india ink on paper, 22.5 x 14 cm

72 *(illus. page 91)*
Costume design for a man in blue top hat in *Skating Rink*, 1921
Graphite, gouache, and india ink on paper, 25 x 16 cm

73
Costume design for a man in striped jersey and checked cap in *Skating Rink*, 1921
Graphite, gouache, and india ink on paper, 23 x 13 cm

74 *(illus. page 89)*
Costume design for a sailor in blue and red in *Skating Rink*, 1921
Graphite, gouache, and ink wash on paper, 25 x 17 cm

75 *(illus. page 94)*
Costume design for Jean Börlin as the Madman in *Skating Rink*, 1921
Graphite, watercolor, and india ink on paper, 30 x 18 cm

76 *(illus. page 90)*
Costume design for a woman in checked skirt in *Skating Rink*, 1921
Graphite, watercolor, gouache, and india ink on paper, 25 x 16 cm

77
Curtain design for *La Création du monde*, 1923
Graphite, watercolor, gouache, and india ink on paper, 41 x 56 cm

78 *(illus. page 98)*
Backdrop design for *La Création du monde*, 1923
Graphite, watercolor, gouache, and india ink on paper, 41 x 54 cm

79 *(illus. cover, page 99)*
Set design with three godlike figures for *La Création du monde*, 1923
Graphite, watercolor, gouache, and india ink on paper, 42 x 63 cm

80
Preliminary set design for *La Création du monde*, 1923
Graphite, watercolor, and india ink on paper, 23 x 28 cm

81
Costume design for a woman in *La Création du monde*, 1923
Graphite, watercolor, gouache, and india ink on paper, 27 x 15.5 cm

82
Costume design for a woman in *La Création du monde*, 1923
Graphite, watercolor, gouache, and india ink on paper, 28 x 15.2 cm

83 *(illus. page 146)*
Costume design for a godlike figure in *La Création du monde*, 1923
Graphite, watercolor, and india ink on paper, 37 x 19.5 cm

84
Costume design for a godlike figure in *La Création du monde*, 1923
Graphite, watercolor, gouache, and india ink on paper, 38 x 20 cm

85 *(illus. page 100)*
Costume design for the First Man in *La Création du monde*, 1923
Gouache and india ink on paper, 42 x 24 cm

86
Costume design for the First Woman in *La Création du monde*, 1923
Gouache and india ink on paper, 43 x 25 cm

87 *(illus. page 101)*
Costume design for a Monkey in *La Création du monde*, 1923
Graphite, watercolor, gouache, and india ink on paper, 34.5 x 19.5 cm

88 *(illus. page 29)*
Costume design for a large figure in *La Création du monde*, 1923
Graphite, watercolor, gouache, and india ink on paper, 44 x 23 cm

89 *(illus. page 29)*
Costume design for a Beetle in *La Création du monde*, 1923
Graphite, watercolor, gouache, and india ink on paper, 16 x 25.5 cm

90 *(illus. page 100)*
Costume design for an archaic being in *La Création du monde*, 1923
Graphite, watercolor, and gouache on paper, 14 x 28.5 cm

91 *(illus. page 87)*
Costume design for a human figure in *La Création du monde*, 1923
Watercolor and gouache on paper, 27.7 x 17 cm

92
Costume design for a human figure in *La Création du monde*, 1923
Graphite, watercolor, gouache, and india ink on paper, 27 x 17 cm

93
Costume design for a large figure in *La Création du monde*, 1923
Graphite, watercolor, and india ink on paper, 44 x 24 cm

94
Figure study for *La Création du monde*, 1923
Gouache and india ink on paper, 35 x 12.5 cm

95 *(illus. page 144)*
Figure study for *La Création du monde*, 1923
Watercolor, gouache, and india ink on paper, 33 x 12 cm

96 *(illus. page 98)*
Figure study for *La Création du monde*, 1923
Graphite and india ink on paper, 35 x 12 cm

97
Costume design for First Man in *La Création du monde*, 1923
Graphite, watercolor, gouache, and india ink on paper, 28 x 17 cm

98
Costume design for First Woman in *La Création du monde*, 1923
Graphite, watercolor, gouache, and india ink on paper, 25 x 14.5 cm

99 *(illus. page 102)*
Costume design for a Bird in *La Création du monde*, 1923
Graphite, watercolor, gouache, and india ink on paper, 36 x 21 cm

100
Costume design for a Bird in *La Création du monde*, 1923
Graphite, watercolor, and india ink on paper, 33 x 22 cm

101 *(illus. page 102)*
Costume design for a Bird in *La Création du monde*, 1923
Graphite, watercolor, gouache, and india ink on paper, 31 x 22 cm

102
Figure study for *La Création du monde*, 1923
Graphite and india ink on paper, 43.5 x 28.5 cm

PIERRE MOURGUE
(French)

103
Poster: Ballets Suédois
Color lithograph, 153 x 114 cm

GERALD MURPHY
(Boston, Massachusetts 1888–1964 East Hampton, New York)

104 *(illus. page 109)*
Within the Quota, 1923
Watercolor, gouache, and collage on paper, 27.5 x 21 cm

105 *(illus. page 113)*
Costume design for America's Sweetheart in *Within the Quota*, 1923
Graphite and watercolor on paper, 29 x 23 cm

EINAR NERMAN
(Norrköping, Sweden 1888–1983 Lindingö, Sweden)

106
Costume design for the Bride and Bridegroom in *Les Vierges folles*, 1920
Graphite, watercolor, gouache, and india ink on paper, ca. 34.5 x 18 cm

107
Costume design for the Bride and Bridegroom in *Les Vierges folles*, 1920
Graphite, watercolor, gouache, and india ink on paper, 33 x 40 cm

108 *(illus. page 60)*
Set design for *Les Vierges folles*, 1920
Graphite, watercolor, india ink, and collage on cardboard, 48 x 67 cm

AUDREY [ANDRÉE] PARR
(England 1892–1940 England)

109 *(illus. page 20)*
Set design for *L'Homme et son désir*, 1921
India ink and watercolor on paper, 15 x 23 cm

110 *(illus. page 1)*
Costume design for the Cymbals in *L'Homme et son désir*, 1921
Watercolor and metallic paint on blue paper, 13 x 20 cm

111
Costume design for the Aeolian Harps in *L'Homme et son désir*, 1921
Watercolor and collage on blue paper, 24 x 34 cm

112 *(illus. page 22)*
Costume design for the Bells in *L'Homme et son désir*, 1921
Graphite, watercolor, gouache, and collage on green paper, 22 x 20 cm

HÉLÈNE MARIE MARGUERITE PERDRIAT
(Born La Rochelle, France 1894–?)

113
Set design for *Marchand d'oiseaux*, 1923
Gouache on paper affixed to paper, 30 x 35.5 cm

114 *(illus. page 58)*
Costume design for the Young Bird Seller in *Marchand d'oiseaux*, 1923
India ink and gouache on paper, 43 x 31 cm

115
Costume design for the Masked and the Unmasked in *Marchand d'oiseaux*, 1923
India ink and gouache on paper, 35 x 41.5 cm

116
Costume design for the Elder Sister in *Marchand d'oiseaux*, 1923
Graphite and gouache on paper, 42.5 x 28.5 cm

FRANCIS PICABIA
(Paris, France 1878–1953 Paris, France)

117 *(illus. page 133)*
Portrait of Jean Börlin with two figure studies for *Relâche*, 1924
Graphite and ink wash on paper, 34 x 27 cm

118
Portrait of Rolf de Maré, 1924
Graphite on paper, 30.5 x 23.5 cm

119
Portrait of Erik Satie, 1924
Graphite and india ink on paper, 22.5 x 15 cm

120 *(illus. page 130)*
Self-portrait, 1924
India ink and ink wash on paper, 26 x 20 cm

121
Portrait of René Clair, 1924
India ink and gouache on paper, 28 x 22 cm

122 *(illus. page 137)*
Curtain design for *Relâche*, 1924
Graphite, watercolor, and india ink on paper, 32 x 50 cm

123
Figure study for a male dancer in *Relâche*, 1924
Graphite and ink wash on paper, 24 x 19 cm

124 *(illus. page 133)*
Jean Börlin in *Relâche*, 1924
India ink on paper, 23 x 14.5 cm

125 *(illus. page 133)*
Figure study for a female dancer in *Relâche*, 1924
India ink on paper, 19 x 15 cm

126
Poster: *Relâche*/Théâtre des Champs-Elysées, 1924
Color lithograph, Imprimerie l'Hoir, Paris, 76.2 x 51 cm

127
Program design for *Relâche* with portraits of Jean Börlin [?] and Erik Satie, 1993 reproduction of 1924 original
Color lithograph, 32.5 x 25 cm

THÉOPHILE ALEXANDRE STEINLEN
(Lausanne, Switzerland 1859–1923 Paris, France)

128 *(illus. page 15)*
Set design for act 1 of *Iberia:* The Port, 1920
Watercolor and india ink on paper, 21 x 25.5 cm

129 *(illus. page 15)*
Set design for act 2 of *Iberia:* Albaicin, 1920
Watercolor and india ink on paper, 21 x 26.5 cm

130
Set design for act 3 of *Iberia:* Festival in Seville, 1920
Watercolor, india ink, and ink wash on paper, 22 x 28 cm

131 *(illus. page 14)*
Costume design for a Sailor in *Iberia*, 1920
Watercolor and india ink on paper, 27 x 20 cm

132
Costume design for dancing women in *Iberia*, 1920
Watercolor and india ink on paper, 26.5 x 20 cm

133 *(illus. page 14)*
Two costume designs for Spanish Dancers in *Iberia*, 1920
Watercolor and india ink on paper, 26.5 x 20 and 25 x 20 cm

134
Costume design for Two Monks in *Iberia*, 1920
Watercolor and india ink on paper, 25 x 20 cm

135
Costume design for a man with a cape in *Iberia*, 1920
Watercolor and india ink on paper, 26.5 x 20 cm

136
Costume design for the Rug Merchant in *Iberia*, 1920
Watercolor and india ink on paper, 25 x 20 cm

ERNST STERN
(Bucharest, Romania 1876–1954 London, England)

137
Poster: Schwedisches Ballett, Berlin
Color lithograph
Private collection, 70 x 92.5 cm

MARIE VASILIEFF
(Smolensk, Russia 1884–1957 Nogent-sur-Marne, France)

138 *(illus. page 2)*
Three program cover designs for Ballets Suédois, ca. 1924
Watercolor, gouache, and metallic paint on paper, each 18 x 13 cm

Sculpture

JOËL MARTEL
(Nantes, France 1896–1966)

139
Jean Börlin in *Skating Rink*, 1923
Glazed porcelain, 40.5 x 30.5 x 12.5 cm

MARIE VASILIEFF
(Smolensk, Russia 1884–1957 Nogent-sur-Marne, France)

140
Portrait of Rolf de Maré, ca. 1924
Gold patinated leather, h. 70 cm

Backdrops

FERNAND LÉGER
(Argentan, France 1881–1955 Gif-sur-Yvett, France)

141
Backdrop for *Skating Rink*, 1969 reconstruction for exhibition at the Moderna Museet, Stockholm, after 1922 original
Oil on canvas, 10 x 4.95 m

142
Backdrop for *La Création du monde*, 1969 reconstruction for exhibition at the Moderna Museet, Stockholm, after 1923 original
Oil on canvas, 7.5 x 5 m

Maquettes
(listed by date of production)

THÉOPHILE ALEXANDRE STEINLEN
(Lausanne, Switzerland 1859–1923 Paris, France)

143
Maquette for *Iberia*, 1933 reconstruction for exhibition at the Archives Internationales de la Danse, Paris, after 1920 original
Wood, paint, paper, and cardboard, 46 x 40.5 x 61 cm

NILS [VON] DARDEL
(Stockholm, Sweden 1888–1943 New York, New York)

144
Maquette for *Nuit de Saint Jean*, 1933 reconstruction for exhibition at the Archives Internationales de la Danse, Paris, after 1920 original
Wood, paint, paper, and cardboard, 46 x 40.5 x 61 cm

ANDRÉ HELLÉ
(Paris, France 1871–1945)

145
Maquette for *La Boîte à joujoux*, 1933 reconstruction for exhibition at the Archives Internationales de la Danse, Paris, after 1921 original
Wood, paint, paper, and cardboard, 46 x 40.5 x 61 cm

AUDREY [ANDRÉE] PARR
(England 1892–1940 England)

146
Maquette for *L'Homme et son désir*, 1933 reconstruction for exhibition at the Archives International de la Danse, Paris, after 1921 original
Wood, paint, paper, and cardboard, 46 x 40.5 x 61 cm

JEAN HUGO
(Paris, France 1894–1984 Lunel, France)
and
IRÈNE LAGUT
(Paris, France 1893)

147
Maquette for *Les Mariés de la Tour Eiffel*, 1933 reconstruction for exhibition at the Archives Internationales de la Danse, Paris, after 1921 original
Wood, paint, paper, and cardboard, 46 x 40.5 x 61 cm

FERNAND LÉGER
(Argentan, France 1881–1955 Gif-sur-Yvett, France)

148
Maquette for *Skating Rink*, 1933 reconstruction for exhibition at the Archives Internationales de la Danse, Paris, after 1922 original
Wood, paint, paper, and cardboard, 46 x 40.5 x 61 cm

149
Maquette for *La Création du monde*, 1933 reconstruction for exhibition at the Archives Internationales de la Danse, Paris, after 1923 original
Wood, paint, paper, and cardboard, 46 x 40.5 x 61 cm

TSUGUHARU-LÉONARD FOUJITA
(Tokyo, Japan 1886–1968 Zurich, Switzerland)

150
Maquette for *Le Tournoi singulier*, 1933 reconstruction for exhibition at the Archives Internationales de la Danse, Paris, after 1924 original
Wood, paint, paper, and cardboard, 46 x 40.5 x 61 cm

GIORGIO DE CHIRICO
(Volos, Greece 1888–1978 Rome, Italy)

151
Maquette for *La Jarre*, 1933 reconstruction for exhibition at the Archives Internationales de la Danse, Paris, after 1924 original
Wood, paint, paper, and cardboard, 46 x 40.5 x 61 cm

FRANCIS PICABIA
(Paris, France 1878–1953 Paris, France)

152
Maquette for *Relâche*, 1933 reconstruction for exhibition at the Archives Internationales de la Danse, Paris, after 1924 original
Wood, metallic paint, paper, and cardboard, 46 x 40.5 x 61 cm

Archival Materials

153
Rehearsal schedule for the Paris premiere of the Ballets Suédois, 1920
Graphite on paper

154
Program for *répétition générale* (dress rehearsal) for the first performance of the Ballets Suédois, Théâtre des Champs-Elysées, 1920
Lithograph

GEORGES AURIC
(Lodève, France 1899–1983 Paris, France)

155
Annotated musical score for *Skating Rink*, 1922
Graphite, colored pencil, and ink on sheet music

JEAN BÖRLIN
(Härnösand, Sweden 1893–1930 New York, New York)

156 *(illus. page 97)*
Choreographic notes, 1920–22
Graphite on paper

VIKING DAHL
(Osby, Sweden 1895–1945 Varberg, Sweden)

157
Letter to Jean Börlin regarding the musical score for *Maison du fous*, 20 August 1920
Graphite and ink on paper

ANDRÉ HELLÉ
(Paris, France 1871–1945)

158
Letter to Rolf de Maré regarding the designs for *La Boîte à joujoux*, 1921
Ink and watercolor on paper

ARTHUR HONEGGER
(Le Havre, France 1892–1955 Paris, France)

159
Annotated musical score for *Les Mariés de la Tour Eiffel*, 1921
Graphite, colored pencil, and ink on sheet music

FRANCIS PICABIA
(Paris, France 1878–1953 Paris, France)

160
Letters to Rolf de Maré, ca. 1924
Ink on paper

161
Handwritten announcement for *Relâche*, 1924
Ink on paper

COLE ALBERT PORTER
(Peru, Indiana 1881–1964 Santa Monica, California)

162
Annotated musical score for *Within the Quota*, 1923
Graphite and ink on sheet music

Book

163
Rolf de Maré, *Les Ballets Suédois dans l'art contemporain* (Paris: Editions du Trianon, 1931)

Video

RENÉ CLAIR [CHOMETTE]
(Paris, France 1891–1981 Neuilly, France)

164
Entr'acte, 1924
22-minute black-and-white silent film in VHS video format

Photographs

(archival gelatin silver prints from the collection of the Dansmuseet, Stockholm)

165 *(illus. page 42)*
Rolf de Maré with Nils Dardel as tourists in Biskra, Tunisia, 1914

166 *(illus. page 47)*
Rolf de Maré in the director's office at the Théâtre des Champs-Elysées, Paris, 1920
Photo by Isabey

167
Rolf de Maré in his Paris apartment, 1920
Photo by Isabey

168 *(illus. page 52)*
Rolf de Maré at the opening of his exhibition *La Danse dans l'art contemporain* at the Archives Internationales de la Danse, Paris, 1935
Photo by L. Debretagne, Paris

169
Rolf de Maré, Paris, 1937
Altered photograph by Max Erlanger

170
Jean Börlin as a young boy, Stockholm, ca. 1900
Photo by Atelier Jaeger

171
Jean Börlin as a young boy, ca. 1908
Photo by Hugo Tählin, Stockholm

172 *(illus. page 43)*
Jean Börlin as a student at the Royal Opera Ballet, Stockholm, 1906
Two photos

173 *(illus. page 44)*
Jean Börlin and Ebon Strandin, Stockholm, 1915

174
Jean Börlin in Royal Opera Ballet, Stockholm, production of *Cléopâtre*, 1919
Three photos by F. Peterson & Son

175 *(illus. pages 76–77, 153)*
Jean Börlin in Royal Opera Ballet, Stockholm, production of *Le Dieu bleu*, 1919
Three photos by Ferd Flodin Studio, Stockholm

176 *(illus. page 74)*
Jean Börlin in Royal Opera Ballet, Stockholm, production of *Schéhérazade*, 1919
Two photos by Ferd Flodin Studio, Stockholm

177 *(illus. page 76)*
Jean Börlin in Royal Opera Ballet, Stockholm, production of *Danse celeste* or *Danse siamoise*, Stockholm, 1919
Three photos by Ferd Flodin Studio, Stockholm

178 *(illus. page 78)*
Jean Börlin in *Arlequin*, 1919

179 *(illus. page 50)*
Jean Börlin in his dressing room at the Théâtre des Champs-Elysées, Paris, 1920
Photo by Isabey

180 *(illus. page 49)*
Rehearsal photographs: Jean Börlin and the Ballets Suédois company, Théâtre des Champs-Elysées, Paris, 1920
Five photos by Isabey

Production Photographs

(arranged by ballet)

181
Jean Börlin in *Sculpture nègre*, Paris, 1920
Two photos by Isabey

182 *(illus. page 81)*
Jean Börlin in *Sculpture nègre*, Paris, 1920
Photo by G. L. Manuel

183 *(illus. page 13)*
Jeux, Paris, 1920
Photo by Isabey

184
Jean Börlin as the Young Man in *Jeux*, Paris, 1920
Two photos by Isabey

185 *(illus. page 51)*
Carina Ari as the Second Young Woman in *Jeux*, Paris, 1920
Two photos by Isabey

186
Iberia, act 1: The Port, 1920
Photo by Isabey

187
Nils Östman, Jenny Hasselquist, and Jean Börlin in *Iberia*, act 1: The Port, 1920
Photo by Central News

188 *(illus. page 151)*
Nuit de Saint Jean, Paris, 1920
Photo by Isabey

189
Jean Börlin as the Young Peasant in *Nuit de Saint Jean*, Paris, 1920

190 *(illus. page 18)*
Maison de fous, Paris, 1920

191 *(illus. page 63)*
Jean Börlin as the Prince in *Maison de fous*, Paris, 1920
Photo by Isabey

192
Irma Calson as the girl who catches butterflies in *Maison de fous*, Paris, 1920

193 *(illus. page 68)*
Jean Börlin and Carina Ari in *Le Tombeau de Couperin*, Paris, 1920
Hand-colored photo by Isabey

194
Paul Eltorp and Margareta Johansson in *Le Tombeau de Couperin*, Paris, 1920
Photo by Isabey

195 *(illus. page 19)*
El Greco, Paris, 1920
Signed photo by Henri Manuel

196 *(illus. page 19)*
Jolanda Figoni as the Young Christian Woman and Jean Börlin as the Young Man in *El Greco*, Paris, 1920

197
Jean Börlin as the Young Man in *El Greco*, Paris, 1920
Signed photo by Isabey

198 *(illus. page 80)*
Jean Börlin in *Derviches*, Paris, 1920
Three photos

199 *(illus. page 61)*
Les Vierges folles, Paris, 1920
Photo by Isabey

200
Les Vierges folles
Photo by Stage Photo Co., London

201
La Boîte à joujoux, Paris, 1921

202
Kaj Smith as Harlequin in *La Boîte à joujoux*, Paris, 1921

203
La Boîte à joujoux, Paris, 1921
Photo by Isabey

204 *(illus. page 21)*
L'Homme et son désir, Paris, 1921
Photo by Isabey

205 *(illus. page 71)*
Jean Börlin as the Man in *L'Homme et son désir*, Paris, 1921
Two photos by Isabey

206 *(illus. page 22)*
Irma Calson, Kaj Smith, and Greta Lundberg in *L'Homme et son désir*, Paris, 1921

207
The artistic collaborators for *L'Homme et son désir:* Audrey Parr, Paul Claudel, Darius Milhaud, Paris, 1921
Photo by Isabey

208 *(illus. page 24)*
Group of musicians known as Les Six: (left to right) Germaine Tailleferre, Francis Poulenc, Arthur Honegger, Darius Milhaud, Louis Durey, Georges Auric, Paris, 1921
Photo by Isabey

209
The dancers and artistic collaborators for *Les Mariés de la Tour Eiffel* (Jean Cocteau seated with script) photographed on the platform of the Eiffel Tower, Paris, 1921

210 *(illus. page 70)*
Les Mariés de la Tour Eiffel, Paris, 1921
Two photos by Isabey

211 *(illus. page 22)*
Jean Cocteau narrating from a "phonographic pavilion" in *Les Mariés de la Tour Eiffel*, Paris, 1921

212 *(illus. page 7)*
Les Mariés de la Tour Eiffel, Paris, 1921
Photo by Henri Manuel

213
Greta Kähr, Léon Stetler, and Margit Wählander in *Dansgille*, Paris, 1921

214 *(illus. page 63)*
Carina Ari in *Dansgille*, Paris, 1921

215 *(illus. page 27)*
Skating Rink, Paris, 1922

216
Skating Rink, Paris, 1922

217 *(illus. page 93)*
Skating Rink, Paris, 1922
Three photos: Kaj Smith, Ebon Strandin, Kaj Smith

218 *(illus. page 94)*
Jean Börlin as the Madman in *Skating Rink*, Paris, 1922
Two photos by Isabey

219 *(illus. page 91)*
Paul Eltorp in *Skating Rink*, Paris, 1922

220 *(illus. page 95)*
Fernand Léger and Rolf de Maré at the Bal Musette music hall, Paris, 1921

221
Marchand d'oiseaux, Paris, 1923

222
Jean Börlin in *Marchand d'oiseaux*, Paris, 1923

223 *(illus. page 64)*
Offerlunden, Paris, 1923

224
Offerlunden, Paris, 1923
Photo by Henri Manuel

225 *(illus. pages 28, 99)*
La Création du monde, Paris, 1923

226 *(illus. page 28)*
The artistic collaborators for *La Création du monde* on the set for *L'Homme et son désir*, Paris, 1923
Top row: (left to right) Jean Börlin, Fernand Léger
Bottom row: (left to right) Darius Milhaud, Blaise Cendrars, Rolf de Maré, Maurice Raynal
Photo by Isabey

227
Darius Milhaud and Jean Börlin at a rehearsal for *La Création du monde*, Théâtre des Champs-Elysées, Paris, 1923
Photo by Isabey

228 *(illus. page 121)*
Within the Quota, Paris, 1923
Photo by Atelier Sully

229 *(illus. page 123)*
Jean Börlin as the Immigrant and Ebon Strandin as the Jazzbaby in *Within the Quota*, New York, 1923
Two photos by White Studio

230
Jean Börlin as the Immigrant, Ebon Strandin as the Jazzbaby, and Edith Bonsdorff as the Queen of Hearts in *Within the Quota*, Paris, 1923
Photo by Abbé

231 *(illus. page 122)*
Jean Börlin as the Immigrant in *Within the Quota*, New York, 1923
Photo by White Studio

232
Paul Eltorp as the Cowboy and Toivo Niskanen as the Sheriff in *Within the Quota*, Paris, 1923
Photo by Atelier Sully

233
Le Roseau, Paris, 1924
Photo by Isabey

234 *(illus. page 31)*
Inger Friis as Suleika and Jean Börlin as Khedad in *Le Roseau*, Paris, 1924
Photo by Isabey

235
Le Tournoi singulier, Paris, 1924

236 *(illus. page 34)*
La Jarre, Paris, 1924
Photo by Isabey

237 *(illus. pages 136–137)*
Relâche, Paris, 1924
Photos by DagensBild

238
Jean Börlin as the Man and Edith Bonsdorff as the Woman in *Relâche*, Paris, 1924

239
Jean Börlin as the Man and Edith Bonsdorff as the Woman in *Relâche*, Paris, 1924

240 *(illus. page 139)*
Jean Börlin in a scene from René Clair's film *Entr'acte*, Paris, 1924

241 *(illus. page 138)*
Scenes from René Clair's film *Entr'acte*, Paris, 1924
Four film stills

242
Scenes from René Clair's film *Le Voyage imaginaire*, 1925
Four film stills

Artists Index

Paris Modern: The Swedish Ballet 1920–1925
was produced by the Publications Department
of the Fine Arts Museums of San Francisco.
Ann Heath Karlstrom, Director of Publications and Graphic Design;
Karen Kevorkian, Editor.

Book design by Robin Weiss Graphic Design, San Francisco.
Type composed on a Macintosh Quadra 800 in
Janson, Cheltenham, Cheltenham Condensed, and Nicholas Cochin.
Printed in Hong Kong at Regal Printing by
Overseas Printing Corporation.